D0385581

Eight Giant Steps to Global Domination

Eight Giant Steps to Global Domination

A PERSONAL GUIDE TO FINDING YOUR NICHE, CONQUERING YOUR MARKET, AND TAKING YOUR COMPANY TO THE TOP

Kenn Viselman

MCGRAW-HILL

NEW YORK   SAN FRANCISCO   WASHINGTON, D.C.   AUCKLAND   BOGOTÁ
CARACAS   LISBON   LONDON   MADRID   MEXICO CITY   MILAN
MONTREAL   NEW DELHI   SAN JUAN   SINGAPORE
SYDNEY   TOKYO   TORONTO

Library of Congress Catalog Control Number: 00-134259

McGraw-Hill

A Division of The McGraw·Hill Companies

Copyright © 2001 by Kenn Viselman. All rights reserved. Printed in the
United States of America. Except as permitted under the United States
Copyright Act of 1976, no part of this publication may be reproduced
or distributed in any form or by any means, or stored in a data base or
retrieval system, without the prior written permission of the publisher.

1 2 3 4 5 6 7 8 9 0   DOC/DOC   0 9 8 7 6 5 4 3 2 1 0

ISBN 0-07-136241-X

*It was set in Clearface Regular per the BUS14 design by the
Professional Book Group's composition unit, Hightstown, N.J.*

Printed and bound by R. R. Donnelley & Sons Company.

McGraw-Hill books are available at special quantity discounts to use as
premiums and sales promotions, or for use in corporate training programs. For more information, please write to the Director of Special
Sales, Professional Publishing, McGraw-Hill, Two Penn Plaza, New York,
NY 10121-2298. Or contact your local bookstore.

This book is printed on recycled, acid-free paper containing
a minimum of 50% recycled, de-inked fiber.

This book is dedicated to my dad,
the greatest showman ever born.

Thanks Dad,
for your support from up there.

Contents

Preface:

The Story of The itsy bitsy Entertainment Company

The itsy bitsy Entertainment Company (TibECo) is dedicated to creating great, imaginative safe*haven*™ family entertainment both on and off the screen. With the plethora of violence and sexual innuendo in the media and the negative impact it has had on all of our lives, TibECo's mission of creating true quality family entertainment that is both fun and funny for children and their caregivers has become that much more relevant. The company is firmly driven by its motto. *To be free to learn, Children must be free to dream!*

TibECo was founded in March 1995 by president, CEO, and Chairman of the Board Kenn Viselman. Mr. Viselman was responsible for introducing Ragdoll Limited programs to the Americas, including *Tots TV*, which premiered on PBS in October 1996 and the phenomenal *Teletubbies*, which premiered on PBS April 6, 1998. TibECo was instrumental in the marketing of *Teletubbies* in the Americas and managed it to become the most successful preschool property introduction of the decade, including the number one in selling soft toys, puzzles, videos, games, and books.

Mr. Viselman also reteamed with Rick Siggelkow, the award-winning producer of *Thomas the Tank Engine & Friends* to introduce *Noddy* to America both on and off the screen.

In 1999 the itsy bitsy Entertainment Company opened its film and home video businesses, based in Los Angeles. This division of the company has already announced production of its first theatrical, the much sought-after *Eloise*, which is to be produced in partnership with the acclaimed producer Denise Di Novi (*Little Women, Batman Returns, James and the Giant Peach*). The company also recently announced its second film, *Jeremy Thatcher, Dragon Hatcher*, based on the award-winning books by Bruce Coville.

Mr. Viselman is the creator and co-executive producer of *It's itsy bitsy Time*, a breakthrough commercial-free programming block that premiered in September 1999 and airs twice daily on Fox Family Channel and three times daily on Treehouse TV (Canada), and which is underwritten exclusively by Hasbro. The *It's itsy bitsy Time* format is already being seen in over 20 countries worldwide. Additionally, The itsy bitsy Entertainment Company has just announced a new program partnership with GMTV in the United Kingdom to coproduce *Nini's Treehouse, Adventures in Oooberryland*, which will premiere in fall 2000 as TibECo's first worldwide coproduction.

With offices in New York, Los Angeles, Toronto, Brazil, and Germany, TibECo is made up of professionals with broad experience in finance, marketing, and public relations from some of the world's leading and most prestigious companies, including Arthur Anderson, PepsiCo, Disney, Public Broadcasting Service (PBS), Westinghouse Broadcasting, Warner Brothers, Mattel, and Marvel Entertainment.

Prologue

The Oxford dictionary defines an opportunist as "One who grasps opportunities, often in an unprincipled way." I, however, think that an opportunist is someone who takes advantage of the possibilities that come his or her way. There is an expression that says all is fair in love, war, and business. Personally, I do not subscribe to that philosophy. I would like to believe that I am part of a new breed of business people who understand the importance of integrity and partnership, while not sacrificing the opportunity for advancement. The three things do not need to be mutually exclusive. In this book I am going to declare that I am a modern-day opportunist and damn proud of it.

I truly believe that success can happen for anyone who tries hard enough and takes advantage of the opportunities that surround him or her. I have been extremely fortunate to achieve both personal and financial success in my lifetime. This success was clearly achieved through hard work, dedication, and a great deal of luck.

In addition to business strategy, throughtout the next few pages you will find a series of random bits of my life. I hope that these bits will show you how being an opportunist does not preclude you from being a good partner to others. In fact the two things can in fact be dependent upon each other.

The first thing I want is to make a confession. I have never taken a business course or even read a business book. I am not someone who needs his fix of *The Wall Street Journal* in the morning. In fact, the only two things I read religiously are the Monday and Tuesday purple sections of *USA Today* and the weekly edition of *Entertainment Weekly*. Everything I know about business comes either from observations of my father at work or from television and the movies.

Although I recognize that we have entered into the twenty-first century, I am not really greatly proficient with computers or technological gadgets, but I'm trying. I still prefer to write things down on paper and prefer my Filofax to my Palm Pilot (which is still in the box). And even though I have marketed two of the children's industry's largest video brands, I have no idea how to program the clock on my VCR. I am definitely a throwback to some other time.

As a child, my parents always encouraged me to try new things and as a result I had broad experiences and varied interests. My father was an ethical man who could sell anything to anyone. This is not a skill that should be used willy-nilly, because when I say he could sell anything to anyone I mean ANYTHING TO ANYONE. At one point in his career, he was an auctioneer who sold electrical appliances to the Amish. My mother, on the other hand, was (and continues to be) the consummator at everything she does. At one point in time my mother was the school librarian, the den mother, the car pool lady, a member of the temple sisterhood, in Hadassah, part of the PTA, and the bookkeeper in my father's stores. To this day, I do not know anyone who can get as much done in the course of a day as my mother. I am clearly my parents' son. I can sell a mean electrical appliance and I have been known to cram a day and a half's work into a day.

For the most of my childhood years, my parents told me that I was going to be successful—an awfully big burden to throw onto a little kid. However, it is ultimately how I became Kenn with two "n's." This is in fact one of my favorite stories to tell people, partially because it is so endearing and partially because it embarrasses my mother. How many people get to write a book and embarrass their mothers? This story evens the score for all the times I had to sing, dance, or otherwise embarrass myself at the whimsy of my parents in front of their friends.

Actually, it's a pretty painless story. It was back in the early seventies, and my mother was recovering from some very severe back surgery. The doctor told her that she might never walk again and he had her heavily medicated. I should stress right here that my mother was neither a drug addict nor was she prone to hallucinations. Additionally, at this time she could not sit down at all, she either had to lie flat or stand straight after the surgery. As a result she spent months doing nothing but lying in bed. In order to spend time with her (and pseudo-baby-sit) a couple of my friends and I would hang out with my mom in her room. One particular evening she had fallen asleep and we were watching TV. Suddenly she woke up and said "Kenny I need to tell you something." She proceeded to tell me that I was going to be famous. Please understand that I was probably 14 years old, and I thought that she had just slipped off the deep end. The likelihood of being famous, at that moment, was less than nonexistent. There was not much call for a short, chubby, acne-faced Jewish kid with braces in Hollywood. I remember telling her something like, "that's nice mom." She then proceeded to tell me that I had to do something to my name. Barbra Streisand dropped an "a" and Cher dropped her whole last name. "You," she said, "have to add an 'n'." I couldn't wait to get out of the room. My friends thought she was crazy and I didn't know what to think. Years went by and we never spoke about it. About 12 years later, in fact, I was working for Mexx (a clothing company in the garment industry in New York), I got a call from a reporter asking about a fashion trend. She was going to quote me (the first time I had ever been interviewed), and wanted to know how to spell my name. So I told her, and then thought it would be cute if I told her to add the extra "n." When the story came out, I sent my mother a copy, and her comment was "It's lovely honey, but they spelled your name wrong." She had no memory of our earlier conversation all those years ago. As a joke I have kept it that way every since.

Growing up with a family of strong upstanding parents and three overexcited boys (either as a result of too much sugar or attention deficit disorders), requires you to use your imagination a lot and to learn how to shout in order to be heard. Both of which are qualities that I have been able to master and utilize effectively in my career.

I learned a great deal about the perceptions of others when I was in high school. I was selected as one of eight students in the metropolitan Boston area to be part of a program that focused on discrimination. Once a week for 2 months I would go into Boston (which was an adventure in itself for a 15 year-old). Eight students would meet in a classroom and get our assignment for the day. The objective was the same every week. We had to go up to strangers and ask them different questions. Some of the questions were simple, like "Where is the bathroom?" "Can I borrow a quarter?" Others were more complicated like asking directions to well-known locations in downtown Boston.

We also did everyday things, like purchasing a cup of coffee. Although the "assignments" never varied from week to week, our physical appearances did. Each week we would have to dress differently: once we were dirty, like street vagrants; once we were in wheelchairs or pretended to be blind; once we were clean but had alcohol sprayed on our clothes (after we gargled with something much stronger than Listerine). The varying reactions were extraordinary. I will never forget how differently people treated us. And equally important, how similar the experiences were of each of my classmates. I learned very early on that people rely on the visual sense for facts. *However*, despite rumors to the contrary, perception is not always reality.

Some of my early career highlights include working at antique shows at the age of 11. There was one particularly ordinary event that changed my life. I remember working at my dad's booth at an antique show on Commonwealth Pier in Boston. It was at this particular show that my dad taught me how things are not always what they appear to be.

Picture this, if you will. Two women walked into the booth at the same time, one wearing an expensive-looking mink and the other an old cloth coat. Both of them looked at something quite expensive. My dad whispered that the woman in the old cloth coat was more likely to purchase the item than the one in fur. I look at him and thought he was crazy (but was brought up better than to say that out loud). And, of course, right on cue "clothy" did spend a few thousand dollars in our booth (I remember thinking it was a king's ransom). To make matters even more confusing "minky" did not buy anything. When I asked my dad how he knew what would happen, he said that the woman in the cloth coat wouldn't be looking at the item if she couldn't afford it. The real shocker was when he said that just because the other lady wore mink didn't mean she wasn't "hocked up to her eyeballs" (an expression he used all the time). He taught me the number one rule of selling anything to any- one—YOU HAVE TO KNOW YOUR CUSTOMER. I realize that this might be a simple statement for an adult, and yet at the age of 11, it changed the way I looked at situations from then on.

As a child, I had two heroes: my dad and Rudy Wells from *Rich Man, Poor Man*. There was one particular episode where Rudy Wells was the construction manager for a developer that had just finished building a huge shopping mall. He went to talk to his boss and told him to make sure to buy the land across the street to prevent the competition from building there. His boss's arro- gance and lack of foresight stopped him from protecting his backside. Of course, Rudy bought the land and became rich and put his old boss out of business. I have never stopped thinking about that episode, in fact many times in recent dealings I ask myself if I have purchased the land across the street. I realized right then how even the best-laid plans can be foiled if you do not take into consideration the factors going on around you. No one lives in a vacuum. Equally important, Rudy was able to think out of the box and shape the future.

My dad taught me things through firsthand experience. I went on the road with him (he was an estate liquidator who trav- eled in about 20 states in the country) during my summer vaca- tions from high school. It was there that I learned another extremely valuable lesson that has drastically shaped my way of managing my business.

My dad used to buy brass beds in the South and sell them in the North and he used to buy bronze figurines and crystal vases in the North and sell them in the South. Ultimately, I learned the concept of supply and demand. And yet I learned it with a twist. Of course things are worth more if the demand is high and the supply is low, but what if I could find something for which the supply was high in one area and bring it to another area where supply was low.

Long before I stepped foot in a college classroom I learned about thinking out of the box, understanding your customer, and supply and demand. And despite a proper education, these three concepts became the blocks that I have built my career on.

Kenn Viselman

Introduction

I remember reading a quotation from someone years ago that stated there is nothing more boring than a man once he gets off the subject he was educated in except, of course, if it is the subject in which he was educated.

Who needs to read a book by another egotistical successful business person? As I sat down to write this book, the one thing I was absolutely certain of is that I truly was not interested in writing a book that glorified my past successes for the satisfaction of my ego.

Equally important, I was not interested in writing a book that took credit for the accomplishments of others. I would not undermine or underscore the role of the extraordinary creators with whose characters I have been blessed to work. Whether it is Anne Wood and Andy Davenport for their unbelievable vision in creating the *Teletubbies* or any of the distinguished producers whose characters include *Thomas the Tank Engine*, *Noddy*, *Miss Spider*, the irrepressible *Eloise* or, of course, all of the brilliant talents and characters behind *It's itsy bitsy Time!* Each of these creators deserves his or her own day in the sun.

When I was approached to write this book, my initial reaction was to feel flattered. As I was discussing potential content, all I could think of was my mother "kvelling" as she bragged to her friends about her son's book being published at one of her weekly card games. I went so far as to imagine my acceptance speech for whatever awards my first book would win (like the Pulitzer Surprise, because it would certainly be a surprise to Pulitzer if I won anything). And then ... I started to write the book, and the bubble burst. I felt incredibly embarrassed writng about my homegrown company's accomplishments to an audience that very likely had never heard of me before. I questioned whether or not my limited success would be too narrow to interest a broad spectrum of readers.

After a great deal of soul-searching and rewrites, I realized that despite my lack of fame, I have a great deal to say to the entrepreneur in everyone, whether you work in the mailroom at Morgan Stanley or in the president's office of your own multibillion dollar conglomerate. I quite literally built a multimillion dollar entertainment company in 3 years from the ground up. I financed my company by maxing out my credit cards, while I worked out of my guest bedroom. I now recognize that my story may inspire others to take risks and believe in themselves.

I believe that *Eight Giant Steps to Global Domination* can offer some insight into marketing a company regardless of its size in today's every-shrinking, highly technological, and wildly competitive world. If a person knows how to take advantage of these eight critical factors, she or he can significantly impact the success or failure of a company.

I am a great believer in learning by doing. Therefore, at the end of each chapter, we've created a workshop to help you apply that particular chapter's key factor to your own career or business. By doing these independent workshops, I hope you will find this book more helpful, allowing you to come away from it with something concrete long after the books is finished and collecting dust on your shelf.

In business, I believe that you need to look at your objectives as if you are building a virtual house (please pardon me for the metaphor). You must be selective about what materials you use to build this house. Make sure to use strong resources, because with the slightest sign of volatility a house made of cards will fall down. You need to build upon your basic ideas with a strong foundation and four walls. Your foundation is always your "focus." Regardless of the type of business you work in, your focus will determine its, and your, ultimate success. The walls however, do differ and are dependent on your product or service.

In the case of The itsy bitsy Entertainment Company our foundation, or focus, is the preschool entertainment business. A strong television broadcast commitment is an example of one of our walls. This not only means the right broadcast partner, but also the right broadcast frequency (how many times a week the show can be seen). Adding a strong licensing program with the right partners for toys, publishing, and home videos completes the other three walls of this virtual home. The roof of the house is my favorite—"promotion." I love the promotion part, because it really defines the height of the walls. The bigger the promotion, the higher the walls.

Your virtual house will be unique in its own right. No two houses are exactly the same, even within the same industry. Experience, creativity, originality, and the product or service that you offer help differentiate one house from another. Each chapter gets you one step closer to building the structure you require to achieve your personal global domination—just remember global domination can be a full-time job. Are you up to it?

As a little side note, for several reasons I am not going to discuss the importance of capital in this book. However, it goes without saying that a company must have proper financing, because even the best ideas cannot be realized if the company is undercapitalized. There are very few exceptions to this rule. I mentioned above that I started my company by maxing out my credit cards and taking on additional debt. This was a higly risky proposition and I would have lost everything I owned, if I hadn't been successful. Recently the guys who made *The Blair Witch Project* did it by maxing out their credit cards as well—however, this was another one of the lucky cases. I truly do not recommend the "maxing your credit card" option to others, because if the long hours don't kill you the additional stress of potentially losing everything most probably will. Most people who get into undercapitalized businesses go bankrupt and have terrible debt problems for many years to come.

My father used to say that luck is the corner where strategy and opportunity meet. Obviously over the past 10 years of my career, I have been the luckiest person in the world.

I truly hope that *Eight Giant Steps to Global Domination* offers some insight and hope to its readers. And above all else, I hope this book brings its readers a great deal of luck.

Acknowledgments

Although all of my fears may come true and no one will buy this book, it was an extremely cathartic process for me—so, even if my worse fears come true, it wasn't a total loss.

I would like to take a moment to thank all of the people who were kind enough to be interviewed for this book, because without their point of view this would just have been about one guy bragging about his accomplishments—and I could not have been a part of that. So thanks Alice Cahn, Cheryl Stoebenau, David Niggli, Joel Andryc, John Dunkel, John Lee, Michael Goldstein, Richard Taylor, Rick Siggelkow, Sam Ewing, and last, but not least, my mom, for putting up with my schtick and for spending the time with my trusted interviewers, who kept me out of the loop.

I would like to also thank everyone at The itsy bitsy Entertainment Company for helping to make all of our dreams come true.

Thanks also to David Levine who negotiated vigorously on my behalf. And finally, I would like to thank Michelle Kanter and Eileen Potrock for all their help in putting this book together—and for convincing my friends in the industry to say such incredibly kind things about my work.

Of course none of this would be possible without my family, whose support over the past several years, allowed me to achieve my modicum of success.

Focus

Understand your essence:
A rose is a rose is a rose.

Trying to define *focus* is a little like trying to define love. Everyone knows what it feels like, and yet when you try to break it down in some didactic fashion you end up losing something in the translation. A company's heart and soul are defined by its focus. Nonetheless, I cannot start this book without at least explaining what I mean by the term. Focus is…"A forward-thinking vision which is open to the elements but not distracted by them, and which gives a clearly defined direction for the future."

The United States Postal Service's motto "neither snow nor rain nor heat nor gloom of night stays these couriers from the swift completion of their appointed rounds" is an example of focus. Focus is like a beacon in the night that allows all parties involved to see the goals of the company regardless of how foggy the surroundings might be. Every successful company relies on

1

focus to communicate both internally and externally (to employees as well as consumers) their future direction. This is because
another important component of focus is that focus is not limited
to the here and now. Focus allows for future growth and is open to
the possibilities.

Something that will be repeated several times throughout this
book is that a company's long-term success is predicated on their
ability to maintain focus over time. This statement cannot be made
big enough, strong enough, or too often.

A "focused company" has three elements: image, growth, and
diversification. A perfect example of a company with focus is the
Gap. They have had an incredible sense of focus for the past 30+
years. Starting as a domestic denim retailer in 1969, selling pre-
dominately Levi's jeans, the Gap has grown into a retail giant with
thousands of retail stores around the world. They have expanded
their company with several divisions: Gap, Gap Kids, Baby Gap,
Banana Republic, and now Old Navy. They have achieved this phenomenal growth by taking it one step at a time. Finding their niche
and expanding upon it. The important note here is that each one of
these divisions has a reason for being and stands on its own with an
independent identity. In other words, each division has focus. They
use the strength of their company name and yet they do not rely on
that name alone for their division's success. The exercise at the end
of this chapter will help you identify how focused you are as a person and how focused the company is in which you work.

Global Domination

As the founder of TibECo, I have been interviewed by many different
reporters. At some point in every interview, the same question pops
up: "What is your goal for The itsy bitsy Entertainment Company?"
My answer is always the same…"global domination." In fact, even
from the very beginning (when I was maxing out my credit cards)
global domination was always my goal. This apparently humorous

remark always gets a laugh from the reporter. I guess they mistakenly assume that I am joking. They are probably thinking that I should be focusing on selling and promoting TV shows, and leaving the concept of global domination to the big guys. Any rational person would have agreed with them. The fact is that in the early days, we were so strapped for finances that *Pinky and the Brain* (characters from a series on the WB network) had a better chance at global domination than we did.

When The itsy bitsy Entertainment Company opened its doors, it presented itself with a strong focus. Manufacturers, retailers, broadcasters, consumers, and most important, the media, all understood our focus and gave us a great deal of attention. This attention from the media has afforded this not-so-itsy-bitsy company (any more) to compete with the largest companies in our field. Every article written about our company—or interview with an employee of the company—is worth money. We have received several million dollars worth of free publicity because of our strong focus. This publicity has led to increased visibility of our mission to our target audience. Focus will get your company noticed better than any advertising campaign can and it's essentially free.

Staying focused—paying attention to both your audience and your goal—is the first step to becoming a success. Just like a person, a company cannot be everything to everybody, but a "focused company" can serve its market so well that slowly and methodically it can take on more and more "adjacencies" until it achieves global domination. One of the reasons for Target's or Wal-Mart's incredible success is that they are building their empires slowly and from an extremely focused POV (point of view). One of the reasons Woolworth's failed in America is exactly the same reason why Wal-Mart is taking over the world. Woolworth's left their basic focus in search of something bigger. They changed from a great five and dime store, to try to become some new-fangled version of a "household/appliance/fabric/make-up/clothing store." Unfortunately they transitioned at the expense of the customer. And in the end, their loyal consumers couldn't understand Woolworth's transition and ultimately went to buy their goods at a different retailer. Many other retailers have experienced the same fate by losing their focus and ultimately losing their customers. They had the opportunity to grow, but lost their sense of focus and forgot who they were serving and ultimately lost it all.

Wal-Mart, on the other hand, is so focused that they are now the largest retailer in the world and will soon be the largest distributor of virtually every product you can buy in a department store. Recently, by using a strong sense of focus, Wal-Mart passed Toys "R" Us in domestic toy sales. They now sell about 20 percent of all toys sold in the United States. Global domination cannot be far away.

Vision

What is the vision of a company? And where does it come from? Frankly the vision of every company or brand is as different as their place of origin. It could come from an artist in the creative department as is the case with Nike. (It is rumored that a student created the famous Nike swoosh that is found on millions and millions of Nike items around the world.) Or it could come from the founder of the company. It is not really important where the vision comes from as much as how it is marketed and presented to its audience. The vision of a company is reflected through its corporate messaging. The itsy bitsy Entertainment Company has added a corporate message to its logo, "...made from children's dreams!" We wanted to create a visual image that could help others understand who we are and our corporate vision. Because so many of the products that we market appeal to both children and the adults in their lives, we have added a new message "Growing up is optional."

Success is dictated by your ability to be true to your vision. You know how they say you're either pregnant or you are not—no one is a little bit pregnant. Well it is the same in terms of focus: Either you are focused or you are not. Your company has to believe in its goal and be totally, unequivocally 100 percent committed to achieving it or it will not be effective. The same thing holds true of people—you are either committed or you are not. I have a lot of friends on those high-protein diets and some are successful whereas others are not. One of my friends is constantly complaining that the diet simply does not work. When I questioned him, he said that for the most part he doesn't cheat. FOR THE MOST PART DOES NOT WORK HERE. Thinking small or dreaming big, it does not matter how unrealistic your vision might appear, you need to stay focused. You must stay the course, keep your head down, meet the ball and swing.

Too many companies are watching their competition and not their own goals and objectives. The competition is not what your company should be paying attention to. Business is like a marathon race: It's about envisioning yourself crossing the finish line when you're at the twenty-third mile and think you can't run another step. It's about pacing yourself. If you keep looking back or to the side instead of directing your energies forward you are likely to lose momentum and possibly trip and fall.

A company's focus begins with a clear and concise mission statement. A mission statement is more than a feel good statement. It must project the philosophies, opinions, and commitments of the company. And equally important, it must protect the company from its archenemy—a disease called *ambiguity*.

If a mission statement cannot be explained in one sentence then question the validity of its focus. When I started The itsy bitsy Entertainment Company, I drafted a very simple and precise mission statement to market great entertainment to young children (under 6) and their caregivers both on and off the screen around the world. Even though it has been 5 years since the company started, our mission statement does not need to be changed or altered. Our focus has never strayed. Despite adversity and a variety of outside influences and temptations, we have continued to focus our company through strong marketing initiatives with a goal of global domination. It is much easier to market a company or its products if the goal of the company is clearly thought out and expressed in a mission statement.

In the early days, people thought I was committing professional suicide by starting a company that specialized in preschool entertainment. Although for the most part people were just trying to help me, they were incredibly negative. I never let this negativity interfere with my focus. I was determined to surround myself with positive, supportive people. From time to time the "naysayers" managed to throw a negative comment my way, and I would dust myself off and keep on going. The question I heard most was, "How could you expect to make a lot of money from people who don't even get an allowance yet?" Even now, the naysayers are still out there. In fact, if my experience is anything to go by, the negative influences will never go away.

No matter what type of business you run or what type of product you are introducing to the market, there will always be someone or some group that will bring negativity and doubt to the project. You cannot allow this type of thinking to impact on your goal. Surround yourself with like-minded people who are believers in your goal and create some kind of buffer that keeps the naysayers out. Stay focused. Your strength and commitment will protect you. Focus is as powerful in warding off the naysayers as garlic is at warding off vampires.

It is equally important for each employee to be focused individually as it is for the entire company as a whole. I was very focused when I started The itsy bitsy Entertainment Company. I reviewed the landscape and discovered that no entity was out there creating great products strictly for the youngest of children. Sure, Disney and Nickelodeon were out there, but they were concentrating on the 6- to 11-year-old market. In the meantime, the country was experiencing a second baby boom, and for some unknown reason, no one in business was cultivating projects for the boomers' youngest children. This huge preschool market—one that would by its very nature renew itself every few years—did not have a champion. After further research, it was clear that there was room for a brand for caregivers and their children that could be powerful and full of possibility.

What's in a Name

I wanted the name of the company to be a true reflection of our focus, which is why I called the company The itsy bitsy Entertainment Company and not The itsy bitsy Licensing Company. It was important that the company have room to grow and that at the same time the growth was specific to what we do. At the time, I thought it was really funny that I was opening up an entertainment company with only one employee (me), thus making it a truly small entertainment company. Additionally, I was going to be focusing on the very youngest of children—the itsy bitsiest. And thus the name The itsy bitsy Entertainment Company. I must confess that there was one other factor in naming the company. When I was a little kid my favorite song was "The Itsy Bitsy Teeny Weenie Yellow Polka Dot Bikini." I used to think it sounded funny and I wanted the name of our company to represent funny for young kids as well. I would have named the company The itsy bitsy teeny weenie yellow polka dot bikini Entertainment Company. The problem was I couldn't imagine someone answering the phone saying "Good afternoon, you have reached The itsy bitsy teeny weenie yellow polka dot bikini Entertainment Company. This is _____ speaking, may I help you?" It was so long an introduction that I knew people would hang up on us or start yelling. So I cut the name back and all our receptionist says is "This is The itsy bitsy Entertainment Company," when she answers the phone.

There is another philosophy that says get a name that doesn't mean anything and create a brand around it. Certainly that was the case with Old Navy and Starbucks coffee. The problem with this approach for someone starting a business is that it costs a great deal more to create an identity around something that has no intrinsic value. I remember reading something years ago about how Exxon did exhaustive research when they were changing their name from Esso, because they wanted a name that didn't mean anything in any language. I think that is a splendid attempt to prepare for global domination. However this is not a practical concept for the average business owner.

On a little side note, we have since opened up other divisions of the company: A teeny weenie Production Company and Polka Dot Bikini Entertainment. So now we are technically The itsy bitsy teeny weenie Polka Dot Bikini Entertainment Group, but only in the legal files. For me it doesn't matter, I still get a chuckle every time I think about it.

Image

Now my company had a mission statement and a name, but that was not enough. I needed to set my sights on developing and marketing the company's image. Unlike the TV commercials for Sprite, the popular soda pop, which suggest that "Image is nothing and taste is everything," in our world "Image is everything and taste is nothing" (well, that's a bit of an exaggeration but you get the picture). It has been said that people are a reflection of those they select to surround them. By that example, any message a company sends out is a reflection of their focus. In business, you have to be extremely attentive and aware of your company's image, because the right image can be the key to success. When it comes to marketing, the product is actually initially irrelevant. At first, it is the image of the product that is important. A good marketer can make any product a success because, for the most part, the basic principles of marketing do not change from product to product.

Several years ago I had an experience while I was working in the garment center that could just as easily have happened in any other type of business that sells products or services to consumers. I worked for a company that had the right product, and yet it had the wrong image. The following is what happened and what we did to redirect our business.

The company I was working for was a small manufacturer that made clothes for both young men and juniors (clothing for teenage girls straight up to young professionals). The company's head design facilities were based in Holland and therefore the clothing tended to have a strong European influence. In the early days, the company was struggling to achieve 4 million dollars annually, and I was hired to do their marketing. Actually I was more like the company's Paul Revere. It was my job to communicate the company's image to the outside world.

Fortunately, I did not have to ride a horse carrying lanterns. I did, however, manage their press, the ad buys, and the interaction with retailers and virtually all other third-party communications regarding the branding of their products. Because it was a small company with limited monies, we had to be clever about how we utilized our marketing funds. At the time I joined the company, their ad buys where being split between their two divisions, Moustache (men) and Emmanuelle (women), and neither was penetrating the market. Both of these divisions depicted a lifestyle that represented forward-thinking fashion (avante garde clothing), and yet, although the styling was great, the youths were either not relating to the brand messages, or we were not putting enough monies into our ad buy to penetrate the market. In fact because ads buys for both divisions were not large enough, we were not effective in communicating our identity to either consumer group.

Imagine a small bakery store advertising their child-sized cupcakes and their chocolate crème brullées separately. If they spent all the money on one statement, "Our desserts taste great," and promoted it to the whole family instead of splitting their buy in half then they would have achieved higher frequency and better market penetration.

Now back to the Moustache and Emmanuelle story….With limited focus testing, we found out that potential purchasers thought the clothes were interesting, but wondered "Where do you wear them?" And most important, "Are they cool?" Cool is everything when you are a teenager. It was clear that the company had to do something to help shape its image and to give potential customers a reason to buy. The company's headquarters in Amsterdam understood our concerns and collectively we established a new direction for our brands.

Although the company was very focused about their fashion and about making products of high quality, they were not focused with their consumer branding and advertising. We consolidated the two brands into one that allowed us to put out one message with twice the monies to a broader consumer base.

We took the "M" from Moustache, the "E" from Emmanuelle, and two kisses from the sky ("X","X"). And so Mexx was born. We put out the exact same fashions as before, without so much as changing a seamstress. The only difference was that now our new product was going to be sold as a lifestyle brand—clothes for young, fashion-forward people who live life to the fullest and are willing to take risks. Everything we did conveyed a sense of fantasy and possibility with an undercurrent of sex. Basically all of the ads were the same: A young man and a young woman having fun together in the most unlikely of places. My favorite ad was of a sexy young man and an even sexier young woman (with fantastically styled hair) laughing with an elephant on a leash in the middle of the Champs Élysées in Paris.

I was able to focus our ad buys and send one consistent message to more retailers and more potential consumers than was possible with our previous split-brand philosophy. We then took this unified philosophy directly to the consumer by opening a dedicated retail shop within a retail store. For example, we opened a Mexx shop in Bloomingdale's flagship store on 59th Street in Manhattan and put in our own fixturing, signage, flooring—even the lighting—to create the ambiance that best represented our image. At the time, establishing a boutique was a revolutionary thing to do in the junior's/young men's departments within a retail store environment.

The idea was similar to a cosmetics concession, but this time, for a clothing brand. We built out the spaces and helped with the ordering of goods, hired and trained the staff, and then we even paid half the costs. Retailers were eating the concept up. I was nicknamed "The King of Shop in Shops," and at one point I had to open 45 stores in something like 40 days. Within 18 months the company's revenues shot up to over 240 million dollars. I learned very quickly that image is everything. I also learned something about personal image as well while I was working for Mexx. The day that changed my view of the world happened at Macy*s Herald Square on my birthday.

We were opening a retail space at Macy*s department store in New York City, which was a *huge* deal. I had a meeting to pick out the shop-in-shop location with the owner of my company, some guy from Macy*s visual display department, and Art Reiner, the president of Macy*s at the time. Picture this, I was dressed in Brooks Brothers head to toe and Johnson & Murphy shoes, my uniform of choice in those days. My boss's dress was typical of the garment industry—an unbuttoned silk shirt with gold chains. Mr. Reiner was wearing a very nice suit and the guy from visual display was dressed funkily with purple and orange hair and several earrings in both ears, the whole nine yards (nose rings and tattoos were not fashionable in those days or he would have had those too). So the four of us are on the junior's floor discussing floor space and where to put the shop.

I had a good feeling for traffic flow and visibility and gave an informed professional opinion as to why I believed the shop should be in the right corner of the floor. The purple-haired guy thought the left corner would be better. To this day I still can't believe what happened. Mr. Reiner looked at both the purple-haired guy and me and back to the purple-haired guy and back to me and to my horror he said to me, "You don't look creative, he does (pointing to the deviant with orange and purple hair). I think we should put the shop on the left-hand side instead." And with that it was done. The shop ended up in the left corner. I left the meeting, and was amazed at how the decision was made. Without a moment's hesitation, I left Macy*s and went downtown to Seventh Avenue South in New York City to a place called With or Without Pain and pierced both of my ears, and I have never put on a Brooks Brothers suit again. I recognized that if I wanted to be thought of as creative, I had to look the part.

Image and perception are two powerful tools that can be manipulated to one's advantage. As a little side note, the shop did great despite my frustrations, and I told the guy at the ear-piecing place "no pain," figuring I was in enough already.

Corporate image is "A distinct perception of a company or its product(s) by a third party." It is important to realize that image is not actually based in fact, but in perception. Do we really believe that Guess? makes a better pair of jeans than Levi's? Or that Perdue makes a better chicken? These long-term brands have a unique approach and image which is why they continue to thrive. For long-term success, it is important to create an image that can be owned—one that is clearly distinct from anything else. The way a company markets its products will ultimately decide the impact and success of its image.

Growth

I left the garment center after working for one other company whose revenues also went through the roof. The business shot up from 12 million dollars to 360 million dollars in less time than you can say WOW. Multiples was a woman's clothing company that packaged its clothes in plastic bags. It was a novel concept that took off. And once again I was there to bask in the glory of its success. This time around I had created a new image for myself—I no longer wore suits to work. Instead, I wore fashion-forward designers and a lot of black. When I went to meet with the visual display guys, they thought I was one of them. It wasn't that suddenly I was brilliant or that I was able to read into the future (those things didn't happen until later), it was simply that now I looked like someone who understood the creative world. As a result of my ability to communicate with both creative people and businesspeople, I was rapidly becoming intimately involved in many aspects of our business.

Once the business took off and became a huge hit, I was asked to start up a think tank for the company. I was given a separate office space for just the owner and myself and was suddenly being touted as the kid with the Midas touch, a step up from the "King of Shop in Shops." Truth be told I just happened to be in the right place at the right time and I knew how to identify an opportunity and take advantage of it.

In 1989, the business started to drop off. Things started to change drastically, and I found the people I was working with to be less focused on their work and more concerned with other factors. I was feeling unfulfilled and decided to leave the garment industry. All I wanted was to be able to make something of high quality. I wanted to explore my vision and "drive the ship." In addition, I was bored and wanted a new challenge.

In the fall of 1990, I was given the opportunity to work in the children's entertainment industry. It was never a part of my broad stroke plan and yet it felt like a really delicious opportunity for me nonetheless. I went to work for QFE to develop the marketing strategies for *Thomas the Tank Engine*. I have been honored with the dubious distinction of marketing the first wildly successful imported children's character in the United States. Britt Allcroft's *Thomas the Tank Engine* did eventually become an enormous success on this side of the sea, although there were moments especially at the beginning where his failure was easier to predict than his success. If I were more of a betting man even I would have bet against me.

In my first real experience in licensing I was forced to either sink or swim in the pool of focus. Here was the situation; QFE (which used to stand for Quality Family Entertainment and was later changed to Britt Allcroft, Inc.—a long story) hired me as their head of sales and marketing. I should have understood right then that there was going to be a language barrier and an uphill struggle. Who ever heard of a title head of marketing? Friends in the industry were constantly joking—where is the Leg of Creative Services or the Arm of Legal Affairs? Anyway, I digress. The story is quite a typical one. *Thomas the Tank Engine & Friends* (TTE&F) was a relatively successful property in the United Kingdom and the property owners wanted to take advantage of that success in other territories. Their most logical step was to bring TTE&F to the States because it is the largest market in the free world and its inhabitants speak the same language (sort of).

Although the creators of the TV series did think of a different way to present TTE&F on the television screen, they did not consider the differences in the retail marketplace. TTE&F needed to be marketed differently off the screen from their strategy in the United Kingdom as well. By the time this was realized, it was almost too late—a lot of damage had been done.

In order to fully understand the situation you need to know a couple of very basic facts about television broadcasting in the United Kingdom. It is always difficult for non-Brits to understand that programs in the United Kingdom do not necessarily run 30 or 60 minutes in length. In the case of TTE&F, it was only a 5-minute program in England (and the rest of the English-speaking world for that matter). In its heyday TTE&F ran only two episodes back-to-back on Mondays at 3:50 P.M. for approximately 10 minutes. That type of broadcasting could never work in America or many other countries around the world, and Britt (to her credit) was quick to realize that television worked differently here than in the United Kingdom. Britt had hired Rick Siggelkow as the head of production, (don't get me started again), an accomplished producer working at WNET (the New York PBS affiliate) to create a wraparound show for the successful 5-minute animations that were airing in the United Kingdom. Together they created the series called *Shining Time Station*. Basically they added a 20-minute live-action wrap to the brilliant animations.

The problem is that they did not consider that the entertainment off the screen in America is just as different as the entertainment on the screen. Without dragging out this story too long, QFE had negotiated a joint venture with a toy manufacturer and a toy sales rep firm. A very logical idea, however they didn't take into consideration PBS's audience reach or their demographics or basically any other issues that would impact which distribution outlets to sell to or how many units to sell. They imported the products from the United Kingdom exactly as they were being sold there without correcting or adapting the products in any way for the U.S. market. To cut to the chase, they sold too many of the wrong toys to the wrong retailer at the wrong price in the wrong packages. Other than that it was perfect. Talk about blurred vision.

Rick Siggelkow, who created *Shining Time Station* offered to share his side of what actually happened....

Actually it's a great story. What happened was this: I was a producer under contract with WNET [the PBS affiliate in New York]. *The head of WNET, Jay Islin, had gone to a dinner party up on the east side and somebody there had just gotten back from England. They had a connection to this new show in England called Thomas the Tank Engine, and they said we think it's something you guys should be interested in for the United States. They gave him a cassette and somehow it ended up with me because nobody knew what to do with it. Everybody was saying that kids weren't going to like it, they want spaceships, they want superheroes....This was the year of "Transformers" craze. They want big things to transform, they want robots.*

I took Thomas out to several elementary schools and I realized that kids did really like it. It was just younger, it was going to skew younger than people were used to thinking because in those days kids shows weren't really broken out from the two to fives to the six to elevens. It was just kids. And besides, advertisers didn't really care that much about the preschool market. It was a new market to people, they really wanted to move the action toys and that's where people's heads were. So then, I got a hold of Britt Allcroft who had the rights and was developing the show

*and she had just gotten Ringo Starr attached to it so I fig-
ured there was something, maybe there was something
kind of big to this.*

*She came over to New York, we met, we hit it off and I
explained to her that she couldn't just put Thomas on as a
5-minute segment, that it had to be in a larger format in
order for it to work with PBS. That some of the values in
Thomas were wrong; we were going to have to do some
revoicing. And, some of the language was wrong and it just
needed to be "Americanized" to work over here. We then
formed a partnership to create a show, and to make a long
story short that show was* Shining Time Station, *which was
really a new kind of format. We were wrapping, I don't like
to call it wrap around, but we were essentially wrapping a
larger story around Thomas. Thomas was the core of the
show, but then there were all of these other things happening around Thomas, which made it a full half-hour show
and also made it work for the United States. And at that
time, there were only two national shows on PBS—*Mr.
Rogers *and* Sesame Street. *Other shows had tried to come
into the schedule like* The Voyage of the Mimi, *which was
very educational, and a few other shows that sort of nibbled
around the edges of it.*

*Nobody had ever made a full run at the national sched-
ule with the idea that they were going to get their money
back by selling toys and videos and books. That concept
was new to PBS, and they were very nervous about the
idea that a show could be tied to merchandise.* Sesame
Street *was doing it, but their excuse was that they'd fallen
into it over the years. But they hadn't started out as a
business proposition. They had started out as a grant-*

funded educational show that just so happened to get into licensing. And Mr. Rogers wasn't into licensing at all. So PBS was very nervous about the show. We couldn't talk about merchandise; we couldn't talk about any of the commercial aspects to stations or to the press. As far as they knew this show had kind of burst on the scene. And at the outset, we only did 20 shows. Now this is where it starts to get into the merchandise end of it. The show was critically acclaimed. It won every award under the sun but we had only 20 shows.

The Britt Allcroft people had gone off and done a number of deals with Ertl, Random House, Strand Video and they'd done it all on the basis that this was going to be a big mass market property because Ringo was attached to it. We got an unbelievable amount of press and there was a lot of excitement about the show. We produced it in New York, so we also had celebrities coming up to the set, and we got great, great coverage. But there were only 20 shows and PBS was only running it on Saturday afternoons because it had tried to create a new block of kid's shows. In this schedule, and with so few shows, Thomas just couldn't reach critical mass and the big retailers like KB and Toys "R" Us, pulled Thomas off the shelves. I remember there was an article that came out that said Thomas is dead in the United States because it failed at the mass market level. Expectations were raised too high and there weren't enough shows and PBS wasn't really strong enough to drive a mass market kind of license at that point. Well it was, but we weren't in a position to really exploit it. So the upshot was the whole thing was teetering on going under, just completely falling apart. There was no real head of licensing. Everyone was just kind of doing it ad hoc. I mean I would do video, because I was television, Britt would do print stuff, and so on. And then they tried to manage it out of England. And they couldn't do it. They couldn't manage the property from that far away; they didn't understand the business cycle over here so the whole thing was just about to collapse.

Then Kenn showed up on the scene. His hair was down to his shoulders. Wild hair all over the place. I think he came out of the garment district and he was very razz mataz. Kenn was actually what the property needed because he understood this world. And Britt realized that Kenny was the person who was going to get them past this point, where you have a show on the air, the show's working, but the merchandise is not selling. How do you get from point a to point b? Kenny came in and it was right around the time that there was a lot of discussion going on with a department store chain called Dayton Hudson. Dayton Hudson is a big midwestern chain of department stores. I think this is before they bought Marshall Fields. And the upshot was that they arranged to put together a range of Thomas merchandise and called it the Shining Time Shop, which was essentially, a little boutique within the department store. Kenn worked with them in order to make that a success. He convinced everyone to spend some money on promotion which hadn't been done up to that point and then we had a retail success with a legitimate upscale operation. We could say ok, yes it's selling at the mom and pop level but it's also selling at a larger level in all these department stores scattered throughout the Midwest. At the same time we got $2 million from PBS, *which is a lot of money from them, to go produce another 20 shows, and then after that they gave us money to do another 25 to get up to 65.*

Then Kenn really went to work. Nobody had ever brought all the licensees together, for example. Kenn did that. And it was great because the first year maybe there were 30 people. By the time that thing was over we had to rent a hall for all the licensees, we had to actually bring them up to Tavern on the Green, there were so many of them and we had this huge party up there. You could always track the way things that were going by the licensees around at the toy show.

Over the next 2 years Kenn took Thomas the Tank Engine *from what I call the high end to the mass market but also somehow found a way to keep pieces of it at the high end. I'm not quite sure how he did it, but certain categories stayed with mom and pop and stayed with the upstairs clientele at the department stores while other categories went to the mass market. And I can remember going into Toys "R" Us and you'd just see rows of Thomas suddenly. I know one thing he did is he completely revamped the packaging. There was a tremendous amount of confusion about whether retailers were buying* Shining Time Station *or buying* Thomas the Tank Engine. *They didn't understand that Thomas was a character within* Shining Town Station. *The analogy we try to make is that Elmo was a character within* Sesame Street *because everyone knew* Sesame Street *but there was so much confusion at the beginning of this thing that the Shining Time brand itself had never been established. So what ended up happening was the character got sold but the Shining Time brand never really worked as*

*a superbrand. That was just unfortunately what he inher-
ited—a lot of confusion, which he had to sort out. Kenn got
it sorted out in terms of the Thomas packaging, made it
consistent. He got the licensees behind it with their financial support, using their clout with the retailers to get the
profits, to get the product on the shelves.*

*Then Kenn went to work on the promotion piece of it.
And what was great about those days is we were up doing
the show and because we were working in conjunction with
Kenn, he could get people to come up on the set which is
always a very powerful combination. Once Kenn got a hold
of Thomas, it just became like a money machine. Money
was coming in so fast that they just couldn't spend it quickly enough. But then Barney hit, going along the same
route we had, PBS, you know, and they were using a lot of
the same language we had used about being good for children and the importance of the property and so on. And
that was a big crisis in our business because we were just
getting started on the third season, we had 25 shows to do,
and suddenly Barney mania took over. The Christmas
before had really been our Christmas. And that's when the
kids had been mobbing the stores trying to get their
Thomas toys and obviously we wanted to sustain that.
Suddenly here comes Barney who's clearly going to start to
eat into our business.*

*What Kenn was able to do, with the onslaught of
Barney, were two things. First he helped to hold down our
position on air, which we did successfully, and Kenn kept
the retailers and the licensees happy in the sense that there
was continuity on the show. He had to keep coming up
with new ideas and new ways to support the show. He did*

a huge deal with Warner on the Shining Time *videos, which helped, because it pumped a lot of cash in. That cash, in turn was used to promote the property and produce new shows which held down our position on PBS. And I think Kenn also very successfully trafficked the relationships he'd built up over the years with FAO Schwarz, with Toys "R" Us, and so on, and we were able to weather the Barney storm and come out at the other end of it as a "classic brand." Also, that's really where Britt Allcroft had wanted to position the property in the first place. So you could go and you could say, well look at Barney, you know, Barney went up like this and then it fell like a stone, but Thomas is still here, it's still selling, it's still going to be here. Maybe some other categories have gone by the wayside because they were part of the phenomenon as the property was building. But at the end of the day, those core items, the wooden trains, the dye casts, the videos, the books, they're still out there. And that's because Kenn got* Thomas the Tank Engine *positioned as a classic.*

In this instance my goal was predetermined for me. I had to focus on how to get *Thomas the Tank Engine* on track again (no pun intended). I had to look at every aspect of our business to understand what had gone wrong and what options were available to correct the situation. Basically if every door is closed to you, you have no choice but to look for a window. The mass retailer was very upset by the poor sell throughs and they were not willing to take responsibility for overpurchasing. The toy manufacturer had so much money invested in tooling and packaging that they were unwilling to spend more monies to either further promote the brand or change the packaging. The show in America was called *ShiningTime Station* and yet the packaging said Thomas the Tank Engine and Friends. The answer became so obvious to me and yet no one was listening. We had to change the name of the product to *ShiningTime Station* and redirect the consumer to the specialty retail channel. When a grandparent, or any caregiver for that matter, came into a mass retail store looking for a toy from the child's favorite show, *ShiningTime Station,* the acne-laden, gum-chewing high school teen who was working behind the counter would say that they didn't have any. No one made the association that the shelves of marked down Thomas products behind them were from *ShiningTime Station.* If *TV Guide* did not list the show as *Thomas the Tank Engine & Friends* then the caregiver did not associate the two as one and the same.

The business did not start to turn around until after we understood our universe and all of the factors that were in play. We did eventually change the packaging to be more closely identifiable to the American television series. Instead of calling it *Thomas the Tank Engine & Friends* product we repackaged it to be a *ShiningTime Station* product. We started shipping products exclusively to specialty stores, because PBS's demos at that time were higher-income families. We created special (and inexpensive) promotional opportunities for these upscale retailers. We addressed the price points and we hired a specialty retail sales force, whose sole focus was selling products to the upscale independent toy retailers as well as updating them on new products and ideas. My first year at Britt's company, their business sales projections were something like $70,000. The year I left, I heard rumors that Thomas had reached over $2,000,000,000 in retail sales worldwide. The power was in understanding our universe and focusing on a goal. What a turnaround.

For a variety of reasons, I left Britt's company to pursue other interests. I was not sure that I wanted to open a company, however I was sure that I wanted to use the skills that I developed throughout my career. I learned through TTE&F that I love making great stuff for kids.

My company's mission is global domination through great stuff for kids, and I must make sure that each individual project that we are involved with supports that bigger goal. Prior to taking on a new property, I ask my staff, "What is this project's reason for being?" or asked another way, "What is the project's essence?" The answer must be consistent with our broader goal or we will not take that property on, even if it could generate large sums for the company. Short-term profits can effect long-term goals. Once you determine the project's essence, you can develop the brand's strategy, develop your marketing plans, and identify the end user.

Once you have your focus, the best scenario is to get the people who work for you to be focused on your goals—with your vision. You can't just expect that by giving someone a job and a title that they will understand the company's focus. It is your responsibility to make sure that your employees understand the commitment and goals of the company and keep them in mind each and every day they come to work. You need to empower them and make them into leaders for your goals.

I think all of this is common sense, and yet too many companies get drawn away from the very simple ideas and, in turn, lose their focus. Harley Davidson, known around the world for their motorcycles, at one time decided that they were in the transportation business, not the motorcycle business. They started building cars and couldn't understand why their business did not pick up. Harley Davidson had forgotten or possibly never knew their consumer. They had built a brand and brand loyalty among those who loved motorcycles. Some would argue that their business was built around a lifestyle that embodied a rebellious freedom of the open road. This was not about transportation and these were not the same people who bought traditional automobiles. They did not understand their target. Harley Davidson has refocused their basic brand strategies. They have now successfully diversified into other businesses, as a result of their lifestyle not in spite of it. Their core business continues to grow with new models of motorcycles and their expansion of their focus into other businesses that include clothing, toys, models, and even restaurants.

The following workshop will help you identify your focus and how you can express it in one simple phrase. Before you do this workshop, think about your objective so that it is narrow in the widest way possible. That means your focus should not be limiting. The power of a clear focus is that it enables you to grow. At TibECo, we have been able to diversify into several different businesses through our focus on our mission statement. Remember, if you are opening a store you need make sure you know the consumer you want to reach. As you answer the following questions, you'll see how I answered them, which led me to The itsy bitsy Entertainment Company's focus.

1. What is your idea/product/concept /goal?
   To create great stuff for kids.
2. What is special or unique about it?
   It provides a safe haven for them.
3. Who is your target?
   Young children and their caregivers.
4. Why does this product work for this target?
   It is created at a pace and with values that encourage children to use their imaginations.

The following is my company's official mission statement:

> *The itsy bitsy Entertainment Company was created to provide safehaven children's entertainment to the youngest of children and their caregivers offering children the opportunity to be free to learn while at the same time being free to dream.*

That is the foundation of my company and the base on which I was able to build my house. What's yours?

You need to remember that the shortest distance between two points has been, and will always be, a straight line. Many companies will try to go in different directions, above or around their key targets, because they think this will be easier, or it may cost a bit less. What it will wind up costing them is their core customer. Global recognition is a great goal, but will it help your bottom line? Isn't it better to be recognized by the 2 percent of the globe that has use for your product or service? I mean who really cares if people who live in the desert know about your powerboat? Global recognition does not mean global domination. Global domination means becoming the key provider of your specific product or service, to have a commanding influence in your area of expertise.

Managing Expectations

Trust the one you're with.

We have an expression in our company that says there is no relationship without communication. We should amend that language to add that in order for the relationship to be strong, communication is needed to manage the expectations of the other party. It doesn't matter whether we are talking about business partners, life partners, or any other type of partners, ALL RELATIONSHIPS REQUIRE EFFECTIVE EXPECTATION MANAGEMENT IF THEY ARE GOING TO GROW AND BE MAINTAINED.

In my quest for global domination, managing expectations has been the most difficult task for me to master because it has required me to remove ambiguity from my business life. All healthy businesses require effective, direct, consistent nonambiguous communication within and between divisions, as well as to the outside world.

Removing ambiguity is everyone's responsibility. It is absolutely not simply the responsibility of the management of a company—every one of its employees needs to take responsibility for removing ambiguity from their communications as well. If anything, it is management's job to ensure that the employees have the direction necessary for them to do their jobs. Imagine an architect who gave an approximation instead of details on the blueprints of a house—how long would he or she be in business? It sounds preposterous but why is that any different from a company that doesn't give concise information to their sales staff or a business that doesn't share its marketing plans with its clients? Ambiguity in a company is like a virus in a computer, if it spreads far enough it can totally immobilize your business. The bottom line to properly managing the expectations of others is to develop effective communication skills. There is only one effective communication and that is the one that gives the receiver a clear understanding of what has happened or is about to happen.

Think of your business as a wheel with several spokes, all of which have to be in place for the wheel to turn smoothly. In my company's case this means understanding the needs of a most complex cast of characters.

Trust from the Inside Out

Effective expectation management requires trust. When I interview someone I am not interested in what they want to do or be in 5 years, I want to know if I can trust them. I make it clearly understood what my expectations are of that person and their future potential within the company. So far either Dean Koocher, our COO, or I have met with every employee in the company before they were hired, and frankly I don't think it would be fair to either the company or the potential employee to do it any differently. Don Gold, who heads our film division, and I sit down with the writers or producers of our feature films to make sure that we understand each other's goals and objectives, before they are hired. We recently offered a multi-award-winning writer a few hundred thousand dollars to write a screenplay for an upcoming feature film that we are producing. The deal points were completed rather quickly. However, before we signed the contract, the only caveat was that he had to fly to Los Angeles and sit down face to face with me so we could mutually understand each other's expectations.

From our discussion, we established what our expectations were and an action plan for the future. Without clear dialogue and direction this writer would not have delivered a script that met my needs and that would be a reflection of poor leadership on my part. Additionally, we saved a great deal of time in rewrites, because we had a clear focus and clear expectations. Every person who works for TibECo on staff, as a consultant, or as a freelancer understands my expectations and the goals of the company prior to starting a project. If they don't agree with our corporate philosophy then I'd rather not take the project on, because I do not think that it is fair to any of us.

In the past 5 years, TibECo has had extremely low turnover. I am certain that our interview process along with our further commitments to our employees is why they want to stay. Of equal importance, is the fact that we are continually striving to manage each other's expectations. Every week we have a variety of different communications that help keep everyone informed of what is going on and deadlines for materials. There are a number of opportunities throughout the week, from staff meetings to weekly E-mail updates to our open-door policy, for complaints and suggestions. In our art department we have a request form that (when filled out properly) gives the artist an understanding of not only what is needed, but also why it is needed and for when.

Giving the employees additional information about different divisions of our business allows them to feel like more of an integral part of the company and less like an assembly line worker. If one division of the business knows what is going to happen to a project after they are finished or what has happened just prior to them, then it helps them understand how they are part of a team with a common goal. We try to make all of the employees understand their roles in the total picture and how, even if they don't make the project with their own two hands, their commitment to what they do for the company enables them to use their two hands in the first place and, perhaps, on another project. Even though it takes a lot of work to keep everyone informed, I think employees are more motivated and more productive if they understand the important role they play in the overall picture.

It is easier to establish the trust of our employees than those of our licensors and licensees; especially in the early days, it was rather complicated.

Establishing Trust from the Outside In

My parents taught me a lot about how trust is built and that your word is the most important thing that you can give someone. My father, who passed away in 1998, built his business on his word and my mother, to this day, reminds me that trust and caring have a value greater than money can buy. My mother probably still says it best....

As a mother, I guess my biggest contribution was being at home with all of my children. We were ethical and honest and cared about each other. And so that maybe in turn that's the way Kenn feels about other people. And that gives him a backbone.

As a kid, if Kenn wanted to do something, we never said that you can't do it that way. We told him to try it. If it doesn't work out then you can do it another way. But try it your way first. As long as you do it the right way, the nice way. No one gets hurt, no one is put down and everyone is treated equally as best as you can.

Trust was developed due to the fact that "our word" was very important. If we signed something or said that we were going to do it without even signing things, it was done exactly as we said that we would do it. And with all of our three children, that's the way we taught them. This is the way you do things. Your name becomes very, very important. That's what you live by and if you spoil that you can never get it back again.

Kenn idolized his Dad. And whatever he did, Kenn thought it was great. And his dad tried to show Kenny that this is how you deal with people. Selling a product is selling yourself. You sell yourself before you can sell the product. If people don't trust you, they're not going to buy, even if it's a paperclip. But you could sell them anything once they trust you. They would be glad to buy from you or go with you or help you or loan you money or whatever it is that you might need from someone.

I loved them all and only wanted really the best for all of them. Kenn was different because Kenn never needed me to say "I love you." He knew that. And the others knew it too, but they liked it better when I would say it. "Clean up your room and I love you when you clean it up." They just knew that. And he knows it, too. It is important that they're able to express the love that they feel.

I am proud that he turned out to be the kind and gentle and thoughtful man that he is. And most about how much he loves his mother and his brothers. And the extra little love that he has for everyone. He just cares about the employees and his family.

In my previous company and other jobs before that, I experienced a weird phenomenon. With new relationships, your partners are suspicious that you are not going to focus enough of your energies on their projects. And when you do make the project successful, they are suspicious that you are not going to maintain your focus on their brands. It all comes down to trust. Developing a trust between your partners is a key component to managing expectations. In order to develop trust many factors come into play like common goals, cultural differences, and quantity versus quality.

Common Goals

I always sit down with a new potential client and ask them, "What are your goals?" I am only interested in working with people or companies who have a similar corporate philosophy to mine. With regards to my company, they must understand the importance of great stuff for children versus good stuff for kids; want to be around for the long term; and most important want us to be along for the ride for the long term. I met with the president of a company who was looking to make a fast buck regardless of the effects it would have on his audience. He was not interested in making the world a better place for children and their families—just money. My view is that you can make a lot of money and make great things for children and their families. Even if I loved his idea (and frankly I did not), I would not have done his project. Because we were not coming to the project with the same goal, inevitably we would have spent more time fighting than making money.

If I were to agree to a short-term agreement with the property owner, then I would not be able to put in the long-term dedication needed to ensure a long-term success. I would need to make monies quickly, even if it could hurt the long-term revenue stream of the brand. If I have only been granted the rights to exploit a property for 2 years, then I need to negotiate as many deals as possible in those 2 years, even if it is at the expense of the brand. There are always market indicators as to whether a brand is slowing down or backing up. I would have to ignore them and continue to put products out there, because any company needs to make money to survive. I have too much integrity to walk into a relationship knowing that there is going to be a conflict of interest. Ultimately, our partnerships are our lifeline to the future, and a conflict of interest can only jeopardize the relationship in the future. Without strong partners and alliances, in today's world, no company can survive.

If potential new clients were to say that they wanted to make a lot of money quickly, then I quickly say thank you and recommend a different company to them. I have no interest at 39 years of age to go for the quick buck (if I were 79 then it might be a different story). It takes the same effort to do a quickie as it does a long-term project and yet a quickie's revenue stream dries up a lot quicker. You become forced to constantly chase last year's business, instead of focusing on next year's.

This is true of any type of business, once you make a quick buck you are always looking for the next one. In baseball you go for the hit not the home run (or at least that was the law before Mark McGuire and Sammy Sosa—but it still works for the purpose of illustration). However in retail, the buyer has decided to up the ante even higher; they are not even looking for a home run—they only want a grand slam. Buyers are purchasing very narrow and deep. That means that they are buying only very few (one or two in most cases) of the licensed characters that are available to them—but buying huge quantities of the one or two that they do buy. They spend much of their budget to buy one property. Well that is a great thing to do if it works, but at what possible cost?

Instead of buyers cultivating their long-term businesses they are focusing their energies on the here and now. Let's look at a couple of examples of possible scenarios.

1. The buyers bought only one or two licensed characters—what if they bought too much? They are stuck with huge inventory problems and kill the brand for future business. This is clearly what happened with the latest installment of Star Wars at retail. Although it was a huge hit theatrically, the retailer bought so much merchandise that even the power of this

incredible franchise could not keep up with the inventory in the store. I believe that this will significantly hurt the potential of a successful merchandise program with the next movie release. Even though the retailers overbought, they are going to blame their failure on the property and lost sales next time out, claiming that they did not do well with it last time (regardless of how much merchandise they actually sold) so why buy it now.

2. What happens when they are buying only one or two properties and they buy the wrong one? They get stuck with huge markdowns, kill off the brand and say that licensed goods don't retail—talk about passing the buck.

3. What happens when the trend abruptly ends? They are stuck with huge inventory problems and possibly lose whatever profits they made from earlier sales. This is probably what is going to happen with Pokemon—if it hasn't already by the time this book comes out on the shelves. Too much exposure kills a brand.

4. How do they make up for the sales the following year when there is no grand slam property? They don't. And that is the problem with retail today.

Fortunately retailers had a huge hit with the Teletubbies at retail and it continues to sell, but that is not an accident. We have been very focused and we have managed the expectations of our partners by working with them to manage their businesses and the role out of products to keep them from being overexposed and overbought. This has been an exhausting and often a frustrating process of communication.

Cultural Differences

As a result of the fact that we represent property owners from around the world (many from the United Kingdom), we often experience cultural differences.

One of the more frustrating things that we have to deal with is explaining to a property owner how our culture is different from theirs. We are regularly in discussions (sometimes rather forceful dialogues) with a property owner, trying to explain our cultural differences.

In advance of doing the deal to represent the U.K. children's property *Noddy*, I anticipated that we would experience cultural differences. I sat down with our potential new partners and discussed openly and honestly what they should expect. Although *Noddy* has a lush history, he was new in the United States.

Noddy is a huge international preschool property, known in at least 40 countries. He has been loved by generations for more than 50 years, with book sales racking up to over 200,000,000 worldwide (with none of those sales coming from the United States). He is such a part of the culture in the United Kingdom that for years their police officers were referred to as "Plods" (one of the main characters in *Noddy* is a policeman named Mr. Plod). Yet even with all the awareness, this beloved brand did not have any modicum of a foothold in America. It was only reasonable that the property owners would experience culture shock upon entering our market. My partners did not understand at first why we were not making tons of money charging forward with this brand in the United States.

Unfortunately, after having seen firsthand what happens when you bring something out too quickly and too broadly, as with *Thomas the Tank Engine*, I knew that it was in the property's long-term best interest to start with small wins and to continue to build on them. I made it my personal goal to manage their expectations, and as a result of our constant communication with our partner, and their willingness to understand the U.S. marketplace, we have started to build a franchise that will gain in importance over the next several years.

One of the big problems with working with strongly established partners is that they have already created successful systems that have worked for them in their territories. We often have to spend a disproportional amount of time explaining our culture to a client. We recently had a situation regarding Halloween.

Although sales of Halloween-related products in the United States are possibly going to surpass Christmas in the upcoming years, in many countries Halloween is considered a pagan holiday. In fact many of our partners do not celebrate Halloween at all. We spent several months explaining to our British partners why we needed to create Halloween-themed products. We told them that it was a nondenominational family holiday and that it was really a great opportunity for the family to play together. It took so long for them to understand the holiday that we missed our delivery dates and ultimately an entire holiday season. It wasn't until they each came to this country and saw for themselves how much of a family event it is in America that they finally came to agree with us.

Although we speak English in both the United States and the United Kingdom, there are times when I question whether it is actually the same language. After a variety of cultural differences, we started calling what we speak in the United States "American" and what they speak in the United Kingdom "English."

One of the more forceful conversations we had with a partner stemmed around a production that we were doing for our block of programming, *It's itsy bitsy Time!* As I mentioned, prior to working on a project we sit down with our team and discuss our expectations. In the instance of *Charlie & Mimmo* we sat down with our French production partners and told them of our need to keep a strong sense of family and for Charlie to be a curious and friendly little boy. When we first reviewed the scripts we had a fear that they might have misunderstood our direction and our needs. For example the father was always yelling at Charlie and at different points within the episodes the father would actually call Charlie stupid and speak aggressively with him. Joan Lambur, president of On-Screen Entertainment–Televisions for TibECo, and I waved red flags everywhere. We talked to our partners once again and yet they felt there was nothing wrong with the dialogue not understanding that there was no way that we would allow this language to be spoken to a child no matter how acceptable it might be in any other country. After a great deal of discussion and ultimately insistence on our part the series was redirected (Charlie is still a little edgy—but tame by comparison) and this has become the most popular segment in our block of programming.

At times it is hard for agents because they have the management skills to manage the brand but not the ownership and often they have to go out and protect the property from the outside world and that can sometimes mean from the owner itself.

Quantity versus Quality

We have only recently figured out a way to limit the inevitable frustrations that from time to time exist between two companies, even when they both have common goals and interests. The answer is so obvious. Increase both the frequency and the quality of your communications and make the property owners feel more informed and ultimately more comfortable with your management. Unlike the beer commercial that is always struggling with the issue of less filling or great taste, we have to make sure to offer both quantity of communications and the quality of our communications.

As I mentioned earlier, managing expectations was not my best strength. I learned that a lack of clear communication could create a sense of doubt or concern possibly even fear or paranoia. Of course, I would make sure that we would get the job done to the best of our abilities, because that is my perfectionist nature. However, I was not placing enough of an emphasis on my staff of the importance of keeping our partners as up-to-date as perhaps we could have done. Although we were preparing volumes of materials for our partners we were not answering their questions. Which of course is an "expectation management no-no."

We had been sending each of our partners a quarterly report updating them on our progress with their "babies." These reports were so big and so detailed that they weighed more than I did. And frankly, we thought that these communications were sufficient. You would think that the sheer volume was enough to show that we were working and working hard. Our reports were clearly brilliant at detailing all of the accomplishments that we had garnered over the past quarter: retail successes, number of units sold, press clippings, number of new licenses signed, anything or everything else that could possibly brag about how valuable we were as partners. These reports were not, however, giving our partners enough information about our plans for the future. The problem is that we were not listening to their expectations, let alone managing them. It wasn't that we didn't know the plan ahead, it was simply a matter of TibECo not communicating effectively. The property owners' suspicion and frustration was inevitable. They were not sure whether we were being reactive or proactive or what our strategies were for the future.

A couple of months ago, I sat down with Kim Schuster-Winkeleer, TibECo's executive director of Off-Screen entertainment, and discussed this issue which I perceived to be our company's single greatest weakness. Yes, you could argue that it didn't matter what we said on paper—we are a company that gets results. And quarter after fiscal quarter we got results for our clients. But, what about their pride of ownership? Were we (touted as the best in the industry, with a shelf full of awards to prove it) forgetting that our partners were the ones who created and owned these brands? Where we giving them the opportunity to take the ride with us? Why not, weren't they letting us along for the ride? Were we just being selfish or possibly insecure? In the end it doesn't matter how you answer these questions. People want to work with others who are willing to share ideas and information and who treat them with respect. At some point how much money you make for a company becomes irrelevant. It was in that conversation with Kimberly that we realized what was going on. Our company was sending out documents that proved how valuable we were to our partners in the past quarter. And that was exactly the problem. What we were showing our clients was why we WERE valuable to them in the past and not why we ARE valuable for the future. Immediately, we developed a whole new approach for communicating with our partners.

We now have monthly meetings with all of our key partners, whether they are licensees (manufacturers), licensors (property owners), or broadcasters and we discuss everything that is going on with the property. Because many of our licensors are based in Europe, it costs the company monies to fly out there every other month (they come to us on the odd month). And yet, these direct dialogues have been extraordinary for opening up communication channels between our companies and understanding our corporate philosophies. Additionally, our licensors' frequent visits to the States help to further their understanding of our culture.

As a result of these increased communications, we find ourselves having a great deal more trust and support given to us. Our quarterly reports have now radically changed as well. Instead of hundreds of sheets of paper, we simply answer three questions pertaining to the past quarter: What are our three biggest successes, our three biggest problems/failures (we don't always have three of these to write about in a report), and our plans for the future? I should state here that it is equally important that the communications are open and honest or we would just be trading off one problem for another.

As an agent, it is like we are the au pair for the property owner's baby. It is only reasonable for them to want to be constantly updated on what is going on with their child. When they give advice or suggestions, it is because they care and are trying to help.

In the case of TibECo, our partners are actually in many cases from another country. However, cultural differences can even exist between companies as well, even if they are just down the street.

At my company, we often present ideas and projects to others whose corporate culture is much different than ours. Our passion is truly embedded in our belief of our work, and that passion always finds its way into our presentations. I remember one particularly important meeting where we were flying 2000 miles to present *Noddy* to 20 corporate executives at J. C. Penney. We needed to get them on board in order to give Noddy's apparel program a launching pad in America. Closing this deal was imperative. The obstacle was that J. C. Penney had invited almost 30 other companies to present their ideas in addition to us (all of the top entertainment companies and studios in the country). We needed to create a memorable experience for our presentation—one that would stand out. We opted to not go the traditional route. Instead our art department created a set for the show, *Let's Make a Deal,* which my staffers assembled in front of J. C. Penney's eyes. And then Kimberly Schuster-Winkeleer put on the presentation of her life (yes she did fork over $50 to anyone that had a hard-boiled egg with them). Sure the presentation was a little absurd and off the wall—but it was filled with a whole lot of passion. Passion is contagious and as a result of our presentation, J. C. Penney selected *Noddy* over all the properties presented to them, to be their exclusive focus for the first 6 months of 2000.

As I mentioned earlier, because we act as an agent for the property owners, we have to effectively manage our licensees' expectations as well. We work with hundreds of companies (some of which are Fortune 500 companies) and managing their expectations may be the most challenging of all of the spokes in the wheel. Prior to signing on a licensee, someone in my company has to explain one basic principle to them. We are responsible to secure brand awareness and they are responsible to secure awareness for their own product lines.

Our relationship with PBS Home Video as the Teletubbies video licensee and their distributor, Warner Bros. (the world's largest video distributor), is a clear example of a strong licensee, licensor, and agent relationship (with the exception of the occasional slip up). The Teletubbies arrived on home video like a speeding freight train on September 1, 1998. The first two videos have been on the bestseller lists for more than 1 year (they are still best sellers list as I write this book). Even with this success, we had hungry mouths to feed...consumers and retailers demanded MORE! MORE! MORE!

The next release was scheduled for February 1999. Everyone already knew about the video line (consumers and retailers alike)...so how much did we really need to promote the new video?

Our answer: MORE! MORE! MORE! Sure, all indications were that the second release would be as successful as the first. And yet, the retail community was apprehensive. Was the success of the Teletubbies first two videos just a fluke? We knew that we had to do something to manage and shape their expectations. Michelle Kanter, Director of TibECo's video and publishing businesses, worked closely with PBS and Warner through weekly conference calls and monthly meetings, to put together an even stronger promotion behind the next release than that of the first two titles.

In the video business, studios create "announce kits" that are used to introduce new videos to the retailers. This uniquely different kit for each release somehow assures the retailer that the distributor is supporting their brand. The Teletubbies had helped to drive retail holiday sales through the roof and we wanted to show how the Teletubbies were going to impact their future sales as well. So...in December 1998 retailers received a music box with Po singing "Twinkle, Twinkle, Little Star." Included in this custom-designed box were the consumer TV and print ad plans for the upcoming video release, *The Teletubbies Nursery Rhymes*. This level of promotion did not stop with the retail community. Millions of dollars were spent on television and print advertising and children had a special treat on the selling floor of the store—a retail display featuring a button they could push to hear Po singing "Twinkle, Twinkle Little Star." The video launched at number one on the video chart and remained there for about a month. (It is also still on the charts at this writing.) In fact each subsequent Teletubby video has landed in the top of the charts. Since their release in September of 1998, the Teletubbies have consistently had a video in the top 10 children's titles (knock on wood).

I believe this business has worked very effectively for a variety of reasons, and yet clearly the exemplary communications between these three companies has been a key factor.

Earlier in my career, when I worked on *Thomas the Tank Engine & Friends* (TTE&F), I met John Lee who was the president of Early Learning Center Stores (ELC was a chain of upscale specialty children's stores). We sat down to discuss the possibility of making something exclusively for their stores. The ELC consumer was mostly upper- or upper-middle class and was clearly the ideal retailer for attracting the PBS audience. We thought the idea of a range of upscale wooden toys would be important for Thomas, because of the price points and the "classicness" and durability of wood. John casually mentioned that ELC was the largest retail account for Brio in America (the top wooden toy manufacturer at the time). As agreed, I met with the then president of Brio to discuss the concept of private label manufacturing a wooden toy range for ELC, and found him to be rather vague and uncommunicative. I wanted to understand his marketing strategy and a variety of other things. He was not forthcoming. I walked away and looked for another source to make these toys for us.

I think I am going to let John who is now president of Learning Curve International, tell you what happened next.

I was running a retail company called Early Learning Center, which was a U.S. division of a U.K.-based retail company. I was based in Connecticut and we had about 80 stores in the United States. As for American toy retailing, Early Learning Centers was one of the pioneers [in the specialty toy arena]. I came on board in 1990 to try to fix a broken retail concept and along the way experimented with several new ideas to expand the market. One of the insights we had, having English roots, was that we were among the first to discover that Thomas the Tank Engine *was a big deal. And because we had 80 stores we were one of the very early larger supporters for* Thomas the Tank Engine *back when Kenn was running the U.S. Britt Allcroft group. Kenn and I had a relationship first as a retail enterprise that provided a good home for some of the early licensed products that Kenn was bringing to market. We were also bringing a lot of the U.K. Thomas product to the U.S. market before anyone else had it. We were an early bellwether for Thomas as a retail company.*

In 1992, I decided to launch a wholesale division to bring some of the private label Early Learning Center product to market. Our game plan was to lead with something really exciting and new and different. One of our ideas for something new, exciting, and different was Thomas on wooden trains. As it happened at the time, we were the largest retail outlet for Brio. We were selling more Brio than anyone else—both in the United States and in the United Kingdom. Even globally we were the largest retail outlet for Brio. So in March of 1992, after a Friday night three-beer brainstorming session, on Monday morning I sent my marketing director, Harry Abraham, into New York to see Kenn about putting Thomas on a wooden track. As it turns out our timing was just about perfect because, at the same time, Kenn was already talking to Brio about the same concept—putting Thomas on a wooden train track. My marketing director came back and said. "I think he's interested." He says it's out of the box thinking. We were a retail company who also manufactured product. We weren't really a manufacturer. So for Kenn to even be interested in our approach was very much out of the box. It was not the safest idea. The safest way for a licensor to go would have been to pick the market leader for a certain category and give him the license and be done with it. What Kenn and I talked about when we got together later that week was that if he worked with us, what I could offer him was the build up of a total brand. All Brio would do would be to create maybe a dozen or two dozen little wooden train skews and call it a day.

*Our dream was to build a whole brand that would com-
pete with Brio piece for piece and would eventually beat
Brio at their own game, because of the power of Thomas.
Now it took a lot of foresight and a lot of courage and a lot
of creativity for Kenn to get that this concept might work.
We were going to create a franchise that would have staying power as a licensed brand. Most licensing is taking an
existing brand, giving a licensor a little subcategory of the
existing brand, and everybody wins for a little while but
eventually it all goes away. Lunch pails, underwear, flash-
lights, key chains, socks, sheets, pillowcases, and furniture.
I mean you name it—it's all the same formula. You do a little bit, for a little while it comes and goes and then the core
brand stays. What Kenn and I envisioned was taking the
best category for a license and building it into a brand that
would be evergreen. Long lasting no matter what happened
with the television. What we knew was that the books and
the videos would be around forever. Thomas's 50 years is
not gonna go away as an intellectual property no matter
what happened with PBS. As it turned out it was true. After
Kenn left Britt Allcroft about a year or two later, Thomas
was no longer on the air [on PBS].*

*We were granted the license and I think we signed a deal
in July of 1992. The license was with Early Learning Center
so I had a two-sided sales challenge. I had to help Kenn
understand our vision and hope that he could think out of
the box and get it. And obviously he did. And my next challenge was to convince my British parent company that it
was a good thing for us to launch a wholesale division and
do something outside of the box as a manufacturer and a
retailer. So I had to also convince them to give me the*

resources and the money to do this. And they agreed to do that. Now later in the year, the British parent company who owned Early Learning Center decided to exit the United States altogether and they gave me a mandate to either buy or sell or close Early Learning Center. So by the end of 1992, I was working on a deal to buy the very beginnings of this wholesale division which was at the time the license for the Thomas Trains and what little business we had. I had to reapproach Mr. Viselman and say, Kenn, I have good news and bad news. The good news is I'm going to give my full undivided attention to Thomas. The bad news is instead of having Early Learning Center behind this enterprise it's gonna be me and my then partner. We would have no guaranteed placement and I would be starting up a brand new company. Kenn had to really step out of the box now. At the time he was well within his rights to say, John Lee I like you, I believe in you but guess what I have to do—the safe thing for the property. I have to go back to Brio and thanks anyway but have a nice day. Instead he said, let's go for it. He said I think you could pull this off. Let's make it work. And he convinced his folks in England, the Britt Allcroft Company, to transfer the license to little old me in my fledgling start-up Learning Curve.

In February of 1993 I started Learning Curve officially and the one and only brand at the time was the beginning of the Thomas wooden railway system which in February 1993 consisted of 29 SKUs [stock keeping units]. We had done about $1 million in sales in November and December of 1992 and all of 1993. After the first real year of business as Learning Curve, we did about $6 million and in the second year we did about $12 million. It's grown since then *and in 1999, just in North America, the Thomas wooden railway brand [was] about a $40 million brand.*

We're not worldwide yet but we're going to be. We're in Australia and have picked up France and Germany. Next year we fully expect to pick up the United Kingdom for 2001 and ultimately wherever Thomas goes, the wooden train system will go with it. It's become an important cornerstone brand within the property. I was not a manufacturer to begin with so I came in with no preconceived notions and no bad habits and sometimes it's good to not know what you should know. Ignorance can be bliss and lead to new ideas. I never had a traditional approach to licensing so I would say all the licensing we've done has been for the most part nontraditional although we are now a nine brand company and much of what we sell is pursuant to long-term license agreements. What's happened as a result of the initial Thomas experience, we just think differently about how to do licensing. We think longer term. Every brand, every product we build we think of a timing horizon of at least 5 years. The second license that I went after once Thomas was launched was the Lamaze infant development system. I approached Lamaze with the same premise. I wanted an infant brand that would begin a relationship with parents at the point of birth. I was a Lamaze graduate and I thought their name made a lot of sense for infant development so I approached them about building a license. The approach was the same, let's build a brand that will be around here for a long time. What's interesting is Lamaze is not an entertainment property but it's a name that's been around for a long time and it's worked well for them and it's worked well for us. The

Thomas Wooden Railway System model that Kenn and I crafted has worked very well.

Learning Curve also does some more traditional licensing. We have two brands. One is called Kid Classics and one is called Felt Kids. Within each of those brands we do some licensed applications on product. For instance we have a wooden puzzle collection. Within our wooden puzzle collection, half of what we sell, at least in SKU, counts as nonlicensed homegrown designs and the other half is associated with current or classic licensed properties: Madeline, Little Bear, Franklin, Veggie Tales, Thomas, Noddy, and Teletubbies. Within that brand we do a lot of licensing and to some extent that's more like traditional licensing. Yet even there we try to think longer term.

In the case of Felt Kids and Kid Classics, those brands behave more like traditional licensing. But with the case of Lamaze and Thomas, the license is the brand. Then we have a similar model. We did a deal with Lionel. We created a new train system for older kids called Great Railway Adventures. That's under license with Lionel. We use their name to give that train some attention and credibility at retail, much as the way we did with Lamaze for infant toys. And there the model is something like Thomas where the concept is a total within that licensed domain and the license is the brand.

When I started the business I knew I would need probably four to five rounds of capital before we could either sell the company to a larger entity or go public. And the first round of money was on me. The second round came from an investor in Chicago who happened to have an existing business. His name is Dick Rothcoft. Dick bought 50 percent of the business within the first year and funded the second and third round of capital. I was looking for a guru for database marketing. And the search for a guru led me to Dick and he also had some money and was interested in being an investor. And not only have we been sucking all of his money but we took all of his time and most of his employees.

Learning Curve offers a parent's club and we have a lifetime warranty for every product. A parent mails in the warranty card, providing us with their names and addresses and sometimes their E-mail. We offer them a chance to join the parent's club for no money and they get quarterly mailings with good information and coupons to buy whatever else is next in the brand. So we send them back to the retail stores. Or these days to the Internet.

I would not have this business today; as it is, I may not have it at all if Kenn were not an out of the box thinker and able to envision a unique approach to building a business. So and time and time again he's proven to be one of the most innovative businesspeople I've ever met, forget about licensing, I just think he's an incredibly clever businessman.

We'll do about $80 million this year in total. The little old Thomas is still half the business. He's still pulling our train.

It does not matter whether you are the market leader or a brand new start-up company, you still need to manage expectations.

The KIS Theory

Communication is the key to managing expectations. It is important to remember the ever-popular KIS theory—Keep It Simple. Communication is most effective when it is clear and concise. Today, many managers confuse our ever-changing technological society with communicating effectively. They believe the technological advances of the twentieth century help them communicate better, whereas in fact often these advances have had the opposite effect on concise communication. Sure, cell phones, E-mail, facsimiles, and overnight packages make communication faster, but do they necessarily make it any better? In fact, since communication is so rapid, it is that much more important to focus on what it is you are communicating. It's also important to remember that nothing replaces face-to-face communication, which is the key to building the relationships that are essential to your business.

At one point all communications used to be face to face. You could look someone in the eye and develop a sense of comfort from each other. Now the world is a different place, and we have many opportunities to avoid human interaction. I think this is dangerous. The key to strong long-lasting partnerships is face-to-face interaction. My Grandpa Moishe used to say all a man has is his handshake and his smile. Now unfortunately you'd have to add cell phone and computer to that list.

This workshop will help you focus on the first wall of your house, whose expectations you should be managing, and the best way to manage them.

1. Whose expectations do you need to manage in order to make your business run more smoothly?
2. What expectations do you need to manage (i.e., sales goals)?
3. What are you currently doing to manage those expectations?
4. Is what you are doing enough to satisfy that person/persons?
5. What can you do to make your communication better?

Use the lines below to write your new plan for managing expectations:

_____

_____.

Separating the Believers
from the Non-Believers

I know he can...I know he can.

Global domination requires at least one true believer. It takes the unabashed passion and drive of one person to make the difference. Earlier in this book I described the post office's motto as focused. Well, in that example the mail delivery people are the true believers. Nothing will keep them from their appointed rounds. Believe me, in many business situations that one true believer has obstacles to get around that are as numbing as 53 degree below 0 wind chills and as frightening as hungry attack dogs. The key to being a true believer is an undying commitment to your dream or goal. In the classic children's book *The Little Engine That Could*, the main character was constantly saying "I think I can, I think I can." If I were writing a children's book to describe the concept of separating believers from nonbelievers, my character would say, "I know he can...I know he can." When I started working for QFE, I was not a true believer in children's entertainment, that didn't happen until it was too late.

Prior to marketing *Thomas the Tank Engine & Friends*, I would never have believed that I would be involved in the children's entertainment industry. My goal, like that of most American business-people of the "yuppie generation" was to make a lot of money, fall in love, and keep stress as far away from my life as possible. Well, one out of three's not bad. It was by working at QFE that I accidentally found something that I loved to do. Making great stuff for kids has become something of a crusade for me. And the funny thing of it all is that I never liked kids all that much. I used to be the one at the movie theater or the restaurant always asking the parent to keep their child quiet.

Everything changed for me in a flash of the moment. It was so fast that I didn't even realize that it had happened. I was in my office at QFE, scheming my next scheme, when I got a call from a mother desperate to speak to whomever made products for TTE&F. And I took the call—which was quite unusual in and of itself. The short of this extraordinary story is that the mother was calling from a small town outside Chicago. She had a 6-year-old son who was acutely autistic. During our somewhat brief conversation, she told me that her son had never spoken and was in a catatonic state many hours of the day, but that he loved TTE&F. In a moment of compassion, I sent her a tee shirt that had just come into our sample room (it was not right—the ink was too saturated, but the mother was desperate for anything with Thomas on it) and a home video. Who knew that from this random act of kindness, his life, his mother's life, and my life were going to be changed forever.

About 2 weeks later I received a letter and a photograph postmarked Chicago. I had no idea who it was from (having basically forgotten about the call about a fortnight earlier). As I opened the letter I sensed something important was about to happen. The letter was from the mother of the autistic child, and said that for the first time in 6 years while watching an episode of *Thomas the Tank*

Engine & Friends, the child uttered his first words "choo-choo." I was stunned. As if that wasn't earth shattering enough, he had put the shirt on as soon as it arrived (6 days earlier) and would not take it off. His mother was forced to bathe him in it and put other clothes on top of his new best friend. She sent me a picture of her son that I keep in my office. I was deeply, deeply touched.

The same day that letter arrived, I received a letter from a different little boy. He wanted to know what was Thomas's favorite food and could he have directions to Thomas's house so that the boy and his family could come over and the two of them could dance together?

I do not know either of these two children and I could not honestly tell you that I keep in touch with them. And yet these two innocent little children taught me something far more important than any textbook about early child development. I learned that children live in the same world as adults and yet they perceive it differently. Children see everything as possible and without limitations. Whereas the adult world is filled with negativity and doubt, children believe that anything can happen. We are taught our limitations not born with them.

This may seem like an ordinary commonsense type of statement and yet even though I was working with a hit children's brand, I never stopped to understand my audience. Well to be fair I did think about whether or not they would like my product but not why. I understood their wants but not their dreams. It was through my new understanding of my audience and by feeling closer to them that I was able to make better stuff. My business would benefit from that new knowledge.

Inadvertently, I was becoming less concerned by how much money I was going to make personally and was becoming increasingly concerned about how the child would respond to a product that I was creating—whether it was a toy or a book or an article of clothing. Please do not get me wrong, there is no altruism in my world, nor was I suddenly going to pack my bags and volunteer at the Red Cross in some third world country. I simply recognized that making money and making great stuff for kids were not mutually exclusive premises. This simple fact has become the mantra of my company and the key to our success.

Unfortunately, while I was experiencing the greatest epiphany of my life, trouble was brewing at Britt's company. Despite all of my accomplishments, I was not being respected for the great strides and growth of the company. It broke my heart that the company believed I was being overpaid and not able to take the company to the next level. I believe they were happy to see me go. So I left with a huge success under my belt, a direction for my life, and my tail between my legs. I was very depressed and questioning my career's direction for the future. Luckily, I had good friends.

One day in late March of 1995, my dear friend Cheryl Stoebenau (a very-well-respected licensing consultant who also has the dubious achievement of being my first TTE&F licensee) called and said that she was going to England to attend the U.K. Licensing Show, and asked if I wanted to come. Cheryl knew, better than I did, that I needed to get away in order to gain a fresh perspective on my goals. She had come a long way on her own, from director of licensing at Hallmark to opening her own licensing company working with blue chip companies in the licensing industry. I think, looking back at it, that Cheryl knew the road I was going to embark on was a very lonely and difficult one and she wanted me to have time to think about what to do next. She encouraged me to go away with her to London. She also knew that money was going to be tight so she took me on an all-expense-paid trip (if she knew that we were going to end up in France and Italy as well I am not sure she would have been so generous). If it hadn't been for Cheryl taking me on that trip, I probably wouldn't have started The itsy bitsy Entertainment Company. I will always owe her my undying gratitude.

Prior to making my decision to go to the United Kingdom, I decided to call a British producer who I felt I might have somehow wronged, and I wanted to talk to her and possibly apologize. It is amazing how humbled a person can become when they find themselves out of work. I had indirectly introduced her work to QFE, although I had never met her. She was creating a lot of children's programming in the United Kingdom, but had not had any success in bringing her projects to America. The rumor mill was talking at QFE and I heard that the deal I had proposed apparently had not worked out. I suspected that we might have done something wrong, but wasn't sure. And that was the last of my dealings with her. So I called to say hello and introduce myself and of course to find out why the deal never happened (a little gossip every now and then never hurt anyone).

I called her offices, and surprisingly got her on the phone. I began the conversation by saying, "Hi, my name is Kenn Viselman and you don't know me but I would like to meet with you." And the ever-gracious Anne Wood said "But, of course, I know you and I would love to meet with you Kenn." We planned to meet for a quick cup of coffee in Stratford upon Avon. So on the Sunday before the U.K. Licensing Show, Cheryl and I went to meet Anne. What Anne suggested was going to be a 1-hour get-together turned out to be more like 15 hours. I have never met a more compassionate and focused person in my life, nor have I had a cup of tea taste so good.

Anne truly believes in her work, her audience, and her mission. She has been creating children's programs for more than 25 years. Although the shows were big hits in the United Kingdom, they had never really been seen outside of England. This is a result of not being able to find that one true believer. I was a huge fan and truly believed in Anne's work. Our meeting on that Sunday was the start of an understanding between Anne and me. I was going to have a direction for my career and Anne was going to finally have someone who believed in her work "I knew she would...I knew she would."

The most extraordinary thing about that meeting for me was that Anne never once asked me how much money we would make (and she still hasn't to this day). All Anne asked me to do was expose her work to as many young children as possible. A promise I was happy to make.

Cheryl remembers our first meeting and then meeting Anne Wood, the cocreator of *Teletubbies*....

I was working with my clients to find them the very best brands and characters for their products. A key element for success in this process is to identify potential licenses early on so that you can get your clients in on the ground floor of the merchandising program. Anyway, the way I met with Kenn for the very first time was that I was seeking a young boy's license for my sleepwear client. I had heard that Dayton Hudson was importing Thomas the Tank Engine goods from the United Kingdom, and that they were considering doing shops. So, I called up and got ahold of Kenn. I think it was either his first or second day on the job. He had not been there very long. We had a conversation and I arranged to meet with him. He was not your typical "licensing person." He sat there at his desk with his long curly blond hair. I think it was in a ponytail that day. You know, there is nothing ordinary about Kenny. We seemed to really hit it off, or at least I think we did. He was very open about the fact that he was "new" to licensing. Because I had been in the industry for a while, we shared information. I gave him some "words of wisdom" from my point of view; and I ended up licensing Thomas, not only for my sleepwear company, but other clients as well. I guess you might say that Kenny made me a "big believer" in the potential of Thomas—not bad for someone just two days into licensing!

Although the Thomas merchandising program had been very successful in the U.K. I believe initially signing on companies in the United States was not so easy. And then Kenny entered from "stage right." I think he really put a good plan of action together, where he strategically directed Thomas the Tank Engine *toward the specialty market. He pulled together a very strong licensing program and did a great job! I think that one of the reasons that the Thomas merchandising program is still around today is the direction that Kenn took with it. He didn't go to the mass market with it, but stayed with the specialty retailers. I think for that time, and with the property, it was the right strategic move. He was very creative and brought his experiences from other areas with him. He looked at licensing, giving it a different perspective. A freshness. He didn't apply the typical formulas.*

Right after Kenn left Britt Allcroft, we went to the U.K. Licensing Show. The previous day to the show, we went to see Anne Wood. We were there most of the day and stayed that evening for dinner. What a great time! It was just so exciting to meet all of the people at Ragdoll and to see their shop and all the wonderful properties they had created. At that time I think they were working on Teletubbies *but it was a very secret, undercover project. They teased us by referring to the fact that they were working on something that was really "unique," but no matter how hard we tried, more information was not forthcoming! We had a wonderful meeting and you could see that Kenny and Anne bonded very quickly. I think that was very important, and this was definitely a pivotal meeting.*

Timing is everything. I think that Anne was looking for the type of representation that Kenn would provide and Kenn was in the early stages of forming his own company. She seemed very impressed with what had been done with Thomas the Tank Engine, *which was originally a U.K.*

property. And she was familiar with the success that the
merchandising program had enjoyed in America. Anne
knew that Kenn was very instrumental in the American
success story.

No Man Is an Island

A couple of weeks after Cheryl and I returned from our European tour, I called Dean Koocher, an old childhood friend. He had been working for big corporations in some form of finance or accounting for more than 10 years. At that time, Dean was living in Louisville, Kentucky, working at Brown and Williamson as their credit manager (managing receivables on 4 billion in worldwide sales). Dean had joined the tobacco giant after working at Kentucky Fried Chicken and EMI Music. I used to tease him about corrupting the youth of today. If the aggressive bad lyrics and high cholesterol didn't get them then the tobacco certainly would. I wanted Dean to be my "suit." His background and physical appearance would make potential investors comfortable. I, on the other hand, had long hair and earrings. Visually we complimented each other. I had learned early on from Art Reiner at Macy*s that people believe what they see. I needed to have someone on my team that had big business experience to satisfy potential investors, financiers, and other big corporations' needs. In addition to his fine suit wardrobe, he was a family man, the caring husband and father of two very young children. Dean and his wife, Audrey, knew firsthand that there was a lack of quality children's entertainment and they both really loved the idea of doing great things for kids. Although he might have loved the idea of moving to New York and starting up a new company, Dean had a family to consider.

The Koochers were rooted in Louisville and he was the breadwinner. Despite the excitement of creating a new company, Dean couldn't just pick up and leave no matter how exciting he found the possibilities. However, he did agree to help out in his free time. Over a period of weeks, Dean used up all of his vacation time and sick days to help me get things sorted out. It was really hell for him. Between the demands at home, at work, and now from me, it was amazing that he didn't burst. Dean was such a believer that nothing was going to get in the way of his commitment to launch The itsy bitsy Entertainment Company. I remember one particular time when I really needed my "suit" to help me at a meeting with some potential investors from Philadelphia (this guy had put together an investment group to speak to us, and they wanted to meet the "finance guy"). Louisville to New York is not a direct flight. The plane was delayed in Louisville and Dean missed his connection. He made it to the meeting, with only seconds to spare. It was like a scene right out of a movie where the bomb is diffused just in the nick of time. Dean felt a lot of pressure, because if we got this deal, then Dean was going to be able to quit his job and move the family to New York. Dean sold his heart out. Dean's dedication to me and our goal reinforced for me the importance of clarity of vision and power of commitment.

They listened to our pitch, but despite obvious interest they were not ready to make a commitment at this time. Dean flew back to Louisville very disheartened

For the next several weeks, on many weekends and holidays, Dean continued to come to New York and work with me to launch the business. Eventually it became too much to bear. On the day that Dean went to tell his wife Audrey that he wanted to quit his job and work full time at TibECo in NYC, he was not sure what was going to happen. The look on his face was so serious that Audrey was afraid he was going to tell her he was leaving and that their marriage was over. Instead he told her that he wanted to start his career all over and that he couldn't guarantee he would have a salary (and he didn't for almost 1 year), but it was for something he believed in and something he had to do. Wow, it would probably have been easier to tell a woman with two young children at home that he wanted a divorce. Fortunately, Audrey shared our vision and believed in the company. It was a tremendous risk for them to take. It was 6 months before the company could afford to pay for a corporate apartment for Dean so he slept on my couch for 2 weeks of each month and spent the other 2 weeks of every month working out of Louisville. A couple of nights he even slept on the office floor. There are many stories in my company of self-sacrifice for the betterment of the company by true believers, but none of them compare to Dean and Audrey's. It was their belief and commitment to me and The itsy bitsy Entertainment Company that helped shape the company's future.

Now back to those pesky investment types. They continued to talk to us for a couple of months. Eventually we believed that they were stringing us along. As was inevitable, our limited resources were running low and we knew that something had to happen. So Dean and I agreed that the time had come for decisive action. They had to come to the table or we had to say goodbye. If they were not interested then we needed to look for other investors and move forward. They were not true believers, and once we understood that we stopped talking to them (I wonder what they are thinking now). As it turned out, the investment group decided to put their money into a small independent film about a wrestling hero rather than back TibECo because, at the end of the day, they believed our business was too risky. Ironically, in late 1995 or early 1996, a very wealthy man from a prestigious family whose film our "almost-investors" bet on was arrested for murdering one of the wrestlers. The movie was never made and I believe the investors lost their money. There are no sure things in life except death and taxes. You need to support what you believe in—not what you think is safe.

I believe every business and every new invention or cure is initiated by one true believer. I understood a great deal about the importance of finding that one true believer when I was marketing TTE&F. There was one particular licensee that turned our business around, as a result of one of their employee's strong beliefs. A true believer.

Before I joined QFE, the company had made the decision to put out as much inventory as possible in the widest market possible. This was disastrous for them. The product was not moving and accounts were asking for markdown dollars and trying to return unsold goods (not a good sign that these retailers believed in Thomas the Tank Engine's long-term success). It was a pretty horrifying first day. I had been in the office only a couple of hours, when I had to start fielding calls from unhappy partners. Basically the brand was over at the mass market before it had even begun.

They were very uncertain times. I knew that the best chance we had to restart this brand was to start small in a very targeted area and build from there. The problem was that toys were not traditionally sold that way. The belief being that the cost of doing business necessitated a role out to the mass toy retailers. Getting a new thought realized in big corporate America is extremely difficult, and I was trying to move mountains. Occasionally you find someone who believes in you so much that they are willing to do whatever it takes to make your shared dream a reality. One such person is John Dunkel, who worked at a toy company called Ertl, the manufacturer of the die cast trains for TTE&F. Ertl had such large quantities of inventory and huge tooling costs that they were desperate to sell goods. John understood that a further role out at mass would destroy any long-term chance of success for this brand. He agreed with my strategy, but all of Ertl's senior management wished to get as wide a distribution as possible, not understanding the great damage that Thomas was already experiencing at retail. John had to fight everyone in his company to make them understand that it was better for the long-term success of the brand *and* for their company to see things our way. A solution that only helps one is not a solution.

John recently left Ertl after many years, but was kind enough to share the story from the manufacturer's viewpoint.

Ertl actually had the license for Thomas for probably 10 years at that time. But just for the United Kingdom. It hadn't come to the United States yet. And I remember the first U.K. Toy Fair that I attended and Ertl actually received the Toy of the Year for the Thomas line that year. It was rather interesting to be at that show for the first time and to see the company picking up something like that. I had worked on the Thomas line here in the States for the United Kingdom. I was pretty familiar with Thomas—the background, history, and everything for it. And so when it came to the United States, I was excited about it because I knew what had happened in the United Kingdom. At the time that we brought it here, Fred Ertl, Jr., was still the president of the Ertl Company and he supported the line, enthusiastically. And we worked with Britt, and Kenn was coming into the picture.

Two things happened kind of simultaneously. When Kenn came into the picture, we were already putting Thomas product into the marketplace and we had two majors, Toys "R" Us and Kmart that picked up on it. But Kenn's position was to pull back because it really didn't have the exposure in the TV markets yet. The television show wasn't stripped and so the familiarity wasn't there with the kid audience, the parent audience, anybody. And it was reflected at retail because it wasn't selling. And that gave kind of a dismal outlook by our sales force and because it wasn't performing. Toys "R" Us and Kmart dropped it. And so we sat with a bit of inventory. And then in working with Kenn we saw what the plans were for the show itself and some of the changes that were going to be made for the U.S. audience that hadn't been made at that point. It was just going to be a much stronger launch. And the changes that started happening at Ertl were that we had a new president that came in.

He changed some of the upper-management structure and by the time that this was taking place, Thomas had kind of bottomed out for Ertl. It was still doing well in the United Kingdom but we looked at what happened with the two majors in the United States and things were just not happening. We had a sales force and a new head of marketing who came in, and coming from a different culture, looked at this as a really insignificant line. It was performing that way. This person looked at it and said why are we even messing with it. Because it was well under $1 million at that time, well under. I was the director of marketing for toys at that time and was working with Britt and with Kenn and I saw what the plans were. And our approach was that we weren't necessarily going to go for the mass distribution but to try to get the free-standing independent toy retailers and maybe some upscale-type toy retailers.

The standpoint of Kenn's direction at that time was that you can take an item into mass and kill it very quickly. Whereas if you take it into specialty it has a longer life. They don't fool around, they don't discount it, they don't close it out at the end of the season. So we signed up to that but then around 1989 Ertl marketing was forced to forecast what our inventory was about $100,000. There were two of us in the department that knew it was performing better than that but our director was just forecasting the inventory. We're going to get out from underneath the license. I know that Kenn met with all of our upper management, our licensing people, CEO, and there just was no interest because of the performance. But they weren't looking at what was happening. We were tracking *this in the toy marketing department because we were watching the Mom and Pops, as we call them, coming in constantly with orders. The product would hit the shelves and it would sell out immediately. Then they would be back for a reorder. We started to fight a bit with the VP of marketing and with the CEO. You know this is a really good license and we should really watch this.*

It all culminated at the Toy Fair because Kenn was seeing the growth in different areas and he suddenly had people signing up for the license. We had a little conference prior to toy fair. And at that point we could consider ourselves the premier vendor or the premier licensee because we had the die cast line and we had a good track record in the United Kingdom. And we had a very extensive line that we could bring into the States immediately. Our hands were a bit tied at Ertl, and Kenn was on the other side saying, "See what's happening." And I attended the meeting, in fact he allowed me to speak at the meeting to the successes that we had had in the United Kingdom and what we were starting to realize with this other level of distribution in the United States. But I still had to convince my management, as did Kenn, that this was a viable license to develop and move forward with. During that particular Toy Fair, Kenn certainly was seeing the interest grow in Thomas and I was also seeing it because I had people on our sales force coming to me constantly saying, "I've got this account here or this account there that needs more product." And they wanted to know if we were bringing out new characters. So there was definitely a lot of interest.

*It was during Toy Fair and a meeting with our CEO
that I felt like I somewhat put my job on the line. I wanted to know what was going on with Thomas. It was going,
we can see, but I knew what they were looking for in numbers. Again, like I say, with the culture and with their
background if a line wasn't a $10 or $20 million line, you
didn't look at it. We were forecasting $100,000. I stopped
the conversation at Toy Fair and said that we would meet
when we get back home, where we can really take a look
at the numbers. When we returned to the offices in Iowa,
we did a quick study of what had come in for orders from
the first of the year to mid to late February. It was rather
surprising because our inventory was nearly gone at that
point. We reached an agreement with management that
we would, on a weekly basis, review the numbers and then
we would order product or bring in product accordingly.
And from that point on it just kept growing. I believe it
was in maybe October of that same year that Toys "R" Us
was in contact with Ertl and with Kenn wanting the
product on their shelves. A decision was made that we
were not going to sell it to them. It was Kenn's strategy to
keep it away from there and really build the strength of
license and not to see anything happen as far as closeouts
or discounting of the product.*

*You can imagine a sales force that sees the possibility.
The person that is calling on a Toys "R" Us or Kmart can
see the dollars that they can generate. We didn't have the
inventory, number one. We couldn't gear up the manufacturing to take care of it. We acquiesced to Kenn and
Britt's decision not to go into that channel of distribution*

but it really helped us, too, because we were able to build a product and support that other channel of distribution. And keep the product very viable.

Being a believer...

From my standpoint, watching the way Kenn managed a license was different than most toy licenses. Because you go in for the big bang, you want to get it in the majors immediately. You want to milk it for all it has for the first year and a half because it is probably going to go away in that short a period of time. Even in the meeting at Toy Fair of that first year when Kenn was on board, he had a strategy he presented to the whole group. This was where he saw the product being retailed. This was how he saw the product being managed. And it was really having some foresight into building it and letting both the show itself and the product come along together. As opposed to pumping a lot of product into the marketplace before it had a chance to really gain its popularity. He was very convincing the way he was approaching the market. It was different than most strategies that were out there as far as a licensed property was handled. We had a couple of assortments and usually a case pack of product the size of the Thomas product would be 24s. So they would take the minimum, and then suddenly we were seeing people step up to the plate for the 144s and 288s as it got into the holiday season and they knew what the demand was. Because they had people asking for the product. And basically in a lot of cases with some of the independents, the product would be sold before they received it. So some of it never made it to the shelves.

> *People had rainchecks and were waiting in line for it, which was very unusual for a specialty store because they don't get the "hot" product. Usually a licensed product would be at mass at the same time as the independent and the independent would hope that through the allocation system, they would end up with product. They would have customers coming to them because they couldn't get it at the mass or discounters because they were selling out, too. It was very calculated as to what product would be coming into the marketplace and what markets would be served.*
>
> *Kenn is, on a personal basis, just a lot of fun. I found him fun to work with and I liked his commitment to the property that he was managing. He didn't back down in the face of anyone. And he liked to see that property presented as it should be.*

Even partners with the best of intentions for each other do not always see things the same way. In my first project for Ragdoll Productions (Anne Wood's production company), I found myself at MIP TV, the biggest European television convention, in the south of France. I was meeting with one of their partners, Carlton, who controlled the television distribution rights for one of Ragdoll's series (but not the merchandising rights, which Ragdoll had already placed with my company). Anne's husband, Barrie (a respected television buyer in his own right), and I had a meeting with Claire Alter, who was handling the television sales for Carlton in America. As the meeting went on the tone started getting more and more tense. A slew of other senior executives from Carlton had arrived as well. I had explained to Claire that I wanted to sell *Tots TV* in the Americas. It was obvious that they had not been able to do it, so I suggested that it would be an opportune time for a fresh focus. Claire was adamant that *Tots TV* could not be sold. She went so far as to say that the *Tots TV* video tape had "more coffee stains on it than any other program in history." As luck would have it, Anthony Utley, Claire's boss at Carlton Television at the time, came into the conversation just at that moment and I said "Tony (to Claire's horrified expression as no one called him Tony) do you mind if I give it a try?" He asked, "Claire if you've not been able to get any interest, what do you want the series for?" Check and mate. After all, who would dare try to match wits with a fool who thinks he can fly? Maybe that was the perception, but perception often is not reality. I really believed in this series and knew that if I could have the opportunity I would find others who believed in it too. When I left that meeting, I felt like the pied piper of quality children's TV.

That fall I flew with Anne Wood and company to PBS with all the rights to *Tots TV* in tow. Anne had an appointment with Alice Cahn, who was the director of children's programming at PBS and Catherine (Cat) Lyon, her associate director of programming. The meeting was a smash, a virtual love fest. Cat told me, years later, that both she and Alice were so taken by our passion for the series, that they knew that they would have to do business with us one day. I was determined to make that someday—today!

I spent months trying to get PBS to commit to this series, and for a variety of reasons they were unable to make a commitment. I was relentless. In April of that year, I went back down to PBS to meet with Alice. After all those months and all that effort, Alice told me that she had seen the tape, but really didn't think it was right for PBS. I was flattened, and yet amazingly somehow during this incredibly difficult meeting, I convinced her to take another look at it. When I called her a couple of days later, she still wasn't sold on the show. So I went into my sales jargon, and explained what we could do to make it work in America. Anne had previously agreed to modify the series for the American marketplace. She promised to keep that in mind and take one more look at it, but this time I asked her to please watch it with children. I knew that

Anne's work spoke to children and that most adults tend to look at children's things through an adult perspective, not a child's. Remember, children live in the same world; they just perceive it differently. Even though Alice has an extraordinary gift of understanding children, Anne's work is, simply put, radically different. To Alice's credit, she did watch the series *again and again,* with children present. This time, when she called, I knew that something had happened.

Alice Cahn, Managing Director, Children's New Media Program at the Markle Foundation, was our strongest ally while working as director of children's programming for PBS:

There were two things that convinced me that Tots TV *was a good choice for PBS and I think both are a testament to Kenn's understanding of the target audience and understanding of the larger marketplace or the larger world in which that target audience exists. I think the change of heart came from a better understanding of the world of Anne Wood, and the genre or the world in which she creates her television programming. The more I saw of Anne's body of work, the more* Tots TV *began to make sense to me. That would not have happened had Kenn not had such an organic belief in the product himself and in what the product could accomplish for the target audience. It made me want to take another look at not only this project but other work that Anne had done. It was the combination of those two things and frankly that really typifies what has signified Kenn's success in the children's business since I've known him.*

I first met Kenn over Tots TV. *He came to our office at PBS with the picnic basket with the table cloth and the napkins and the fried chicken. It was this typical* Tots TV *adventure. He created the Tots TV environment in my office to show me how appealing that environment was and if I found it appealing, why wouldn't the target audience, which I represented, or sought to represent, find it appealing as well? The pitch or the sell really looked not only at who I was and what my needs were, but really represented who the target audience was and how the project appealed to the target audience. Afterward, Kenn was calling me and saying, "You've got to look at it again, you've got to really watch it, watch it with kids. You have to. Kids really like this, I know your schedule, I know what you're looking for. This is a multilingual series. This is a series that looks at language development both English and Spanish. I know what you're looking for, for the whole Ready To Learn block for PBS. I know what will position you well." All of what he said was right on target and was on par, if not ahead of my own strategic thinking about the schedule. He even had competitors calling me and saying, "I understand you're looking at Tots TV, it's great." He had Ken Katsumoto from Paragon Entertainment calling and saying "we're whistling the theme song in our offices here at Paragon." When you watch a lot of kids programming, when I watched Tots TV first, I thought it was really nice. But I don't think I really got it, and it was from Kenn's really heartfelt belief that this was a project and producer that belonged on public television, that we continued to watch and eventually bought it.*

In my initial look at Tots TV with the one or two kids that watched it with me, I didn't get a visceral reaction and I wasn't seeing a bunch of eyes on the screen or participatory things happening. Kenn had such a clear

understanding, not only of who children are but the busi-
ness of children's television and that was what made me
continue to test it with kids. It was having someone say
something that I probably already knew but I was not pay-
ing attention to. Tots TV was different than the other pro-
grams which children were seeing on the air. At that time
I was being pitched by pretty much everybody on a lot of
programming, much of which was inappropriate. I had to
take another look at Tots TV researching how do kids
watch something, how do they get it, and how quickly do
they get familiar with it? Showing kids something that is
brand new to them and having them say I don't like it is
like the first time you taste a lot of foods. You don't like
them either. But then you taste them again, and it's like
"Oh, maybe it's not so bad." And then by the third time, it's
like, "Gee, can I have Rice Krispies again this morning,
that was really good." Again, it was watching Tots TV with
kids that made me see into it. I continue to believe that
Tots TV is a brilliant series—brilliantly written and bril-
liantly acted. I think what drove me to continue to look at
it was the recognition that in Kenn I had more than a
salesman, I had a potential partner.

I knew that if I had not been able to get PBS to take the show, my company might go down in flames, and I hated the thought of letting down my believers. The problem was that there were no open slots on PBS's schedule. I had to do something. So after a great deal of brainstorming, Alice, Cat, and I thought up a way to create a new type of offering to the PBS affiliates. We were going to give them additional programming as alternatives to their exist-ing schedule. At that time, PBS stations were using alternative programs from a service called APS, which was offering them shows that did not always meet the PBS Ready to Learn criteria. Alice, by offering PBS-sanctioned shows, in a special PBS Plus feed, was able to satisfy station's needs for alternative programs. The difference was that these programs did meet PBS's educational criteria. And further, if for some reason a series that is currently being offered in the schedule is underperforming in a particular market, then the programmer can substitute it with the "alternate series." It was a win-win for everyone. The stations got to localize their schedules to fit their audiences, Alice got to create a better way to serve the stations and I got Anne's series on the air. It turned out that I got word from PBS the day before Licensing Show '96 that *Tots TV* was a go and would be airing in the fall of that year. I spent the evening before this important trade show changing my exhibit to make sure everyone knew the news. Whew!!!

Many of the people who know this story say that I willed it to happen, but I think it was more than that. I was able to share Anne's and my vision honestly with people and make believers out of them. I just happened to have the wisdom and luck (opportunity and strategy) to be in the right place at the right time.

Persistence Pays Off

When it came time to get the *Teletubbies* on air, we had attempted to win a grant from CPB (Corporation for Public Broadcasting) and although it was close we lost out to two other shows. Not being one to take no for an answer, I tried a couple of the more traditional routes to sell the series. When they all failed, I decided to take a whole new approach. Alice really loved the series and understood how groundbreaking it was and yet PBS was really slow in making a broadcasting commitment. I did not want Alice to forget about this incredible series or forget to push whomever or whatever was causing the delay. So...

I sent Alice a fax every day telling her that I was going on a hunger strike until she called me with some information. And like clockwork, every single day I would send her a fax telling her how I was wasting away waiting for her reply. They were silly little faxes, which I sent to the general fax machine at PBS. Word had started to get around the offices that there was this crazy person on a hunger strike—and only Alice could save him. (It gave her quite the reputation there.) My notes were simple one-line messages with statements like "I would eat my right arm off for the taste of a knish. Please respond." Or "Please hurry, my mom is starting to worry." I sent her a news story about a guy who over time ate a Volkswagen piece by piece, and how delicious that sounded to me (after not eating for 18 days). It was really important for me to keep things light. I knew that Alice believed in the *Teletubbies,* I just wanted to keep the show in the forefront of her mind without being annoying. I had to send those daily reminders for 33 straight days, until I got word. I knew that this series was right for PBS and that PBS was right for this series. I also knew that it was just a matter of time until they would commit to the *Teletubbies.* But even I did not see the meteorite coming.

Alice remembers my bombardment...

We loved Teletubbies *from a creative perspective. At the time there wasn't any video. It hadn't premiered on the BBC yet, so we didn't have anything to show people. We were really having them look at other projects of Anne's and saying "This is a woman who looks and projects and begins by really seminal questions like, 'What do children know now?' 'What are children's developmental capabilities? and What do I want them to know? What is appropriate for them to know?' 'What are their interests?' 'What are the questions they are asking? And how do I develop television that will meet those developmental needs and interests?' I know that the idea of four characters with television sets in their stomachs sounds a little bit out there. But you have to trust me." And you have people look at you and ask why. I was working with Kenn and others to find ways to bring people into the fold, to help people recognize that this was truly going to be a series that would reestablish or help continue public television's relationship or reputation as being a leader in the world of children's media. Kenn was very patient for a long time and then was not very patient anymore. And sent me a fax saying, "This series has to go on your air. This is the only place for it. And until you can figure out how to do this, I'm going on a hunger strike."*

I know that it sounds really goofy now and it sounds friv- olous to even compare it to other political movements where people went on hunger strikes because of their beliefs. But I have to tell you that having worked with Kenn on Tots TV *and having seen the other projects that itsy bitsy Entertainment was getting involved in, I really was a little bit frightened when I got the fax. I mean this program was as meaningful to him as a political or social cause would have been 20 years ago. He truly believes that this project needs to be on free publicly accessible television so that all children will have the benefit of this entertainment and this information. They will have the benefit of watching the genius teacher that Anne Wood is. So I got it and you get that very motherly kind of, oh my God, he's not going to eat. I would walk around the building, saying, "Look this is a producer who believes in the work. How could we doubt the veracity of what he is saying. How could you doubt the pas- sion with which he is bringing us this project and support- ing this program. Look at the lengths to which he is willing to go." And so, it was absolutely the first time and frankly the last time that anyone had done anything like that. And I imagine as Kenn and I continue to work together in the future, he will undoubtedly surprise me with something beyond the hunger strike. It will be something different and it will be something absolutely appropriate. And that is the whole thing, that's the real point here. It sounds so inappropriate, it sounds so over the top. What do you mean you went on a hunger strike and faxed that woman every day telling her how much weight you were losing and how the necks on your shirts were too big. And that you were sort of crawling to the fax machine. It's like how dare you use that, it is only television. But the fact is it was about the show. It was about, you know, what is really going on was someone saying, "I believe in this so much. This means so much and you know who I am and you know what I stand for. You need to see the depth of my commitment and the depth of my sincerity. You need to understand how much I believe that this belongs on the channel that you have the power to program, that I will do just about anything to make sure that goal is accomplished and that audience gets serviced. And, I'm not discounting the fact that another motivation was that my company succeeds. That was absolutely parallel with it." And I don't have a problem with that. Why shouldn't the company succeed? The fact is that what made Kenn different at that time and what continues to distinguish itsy bitsy Entertainment is that if you look at those three strands: makes my company succeed, belongs in the environment in which I am selling, meets real needs and interests of the target audience. Most people really just have the one: this project will make my company succeed, so buy it from me. That is not a very powerful argument but when those three arguments are lined up, you have an incredibly solid base upon which you can do pretty much anything. It is completely analogous when you think about it to how Anne Wood builds her television shows. If you look at the most exciting and creative television, there is a really clear instructional design that is a silent unseen foundation to the creator. There is a really clear understanding of who the target audience is. There are really clearly stated goals and objectives. There is a way of deciding and seeing how you met those goals and objectives. And when that's done , your creative ideas can go anywhere. It can go in all kinds of directions because you always have that touchstone of knowing what your goal is and knowing how you'll know when you've met your goal. And so I think that's the brilliance of Anne Woods' television. It is also the brilliance of Kenn's identification of a producer who no one else was really paying attention to. And he completely got it and made it work."*

You are the first step in separating your believers from your nonbelievers. You need to find the thing that makes you passionate about what you do now or what you want to be doing. Once you find the heart, you need to find a way to share it. You must find a way to communicate your passion to others and find that one true believer. It's OK if it is just one person at a time or a whole group at once.

I have always truly believed in my company's success, and believed early on that The itsy bitsy Entertainment Company would achieve global domination in my lifetime. I had to find people willing to believe in me and my goals, which wasn't that easy considering all I had was a vision, albeit a very uncompromising and passionate vision. There were a number of times that I would just sit in my office and feel like it was all a dream from which I would wake up. I would find all of my friends around me telling me of the horrible tornado that flew through town, and that this extraordinary adventure had never really happened.

This workshop will help you build the second wall of your house.

1. What is your goal?
2. What is special about your goal?
3. Who do you need to convince in order to accomplish your goal?
4. What is special or unusual about that person?
5. What can you do to make a lasting impression on that person?

You will you go about getting the believer on your side by focusing on weeding out your nonbelievers. But always remember that in order to find your champion you must be the greatest champion of all.

Be a Non-Traditionalist

An egg cup makes a very good hat.

—ELOISE

Successful businesspeople are always suggesting to others to think out of the box. But they never say how to do it. There is no rule to tell you how to define your box, let alone how to think out of it. In fact the only rule is that there are no rules. Maybe your box has rounded corners instead of square ones or maybe it is made of water. Thinking out of the box is an expression that I personally feel is overused and has lost its true meaning. All that this expression means is think of nontraditional approaches to a situation. Get out your weed whacker and create a new path for yourself.

Clearly I am a nontraditional thinker, I have created an art form out of it. A large part of my success has been my ability to keep the competition guessing what's next. Under my guidance The itsy bitsy Entertainment Company has constantly raised the bar with each new product introduction. We are always looking for interesting new ways to highlight each property and to establish them as perennial favorites, while allowing them to grow to their fullest potential. At the same time we keep creating new opportunities for our own growth. In the past 5 years, we have grown from a licensing agent to a full-fledged international entertainment company with offices in four countries.

In this chapter, start thinking about what makes you (your company or the product you are selling) unique and how can you use that individuality in your career (or for your project's success or your company's future growth).

Recently, some American-produced feature films have taken a nontraditional approach to film making by using a surprise ending. Two examples are *The Fight Club* and the *Sixth Sense*. Both of these twist what you have been led to believe is in fact reality. Throughout the movie you thought that you were one place only to find at end of the film that you were actually somewhere very different. Sometimes perception is not reality. Of course, because those films are big hits, what is likely to happen is that too many American films are going to have surprise endings and thus spoil the originality of the concept of the surprise ending. Too much of a good thing is not a good thing. Originality is key to marketing a new product and maintaining market share.

I always get in trouble for saying this and yet here I am about to put it in writing for the whole world to see forever and ever: PEOPLE ARE SHEEP JUST WAITING FOR A HERDER TO COME ALONG. Don't be afraid to be a herder.

I remember when Nicholas Callaway, the packager for the *Miss Spider* books, went to Hollywood to present the idea of a Miss Spider movie. At first all of the studios were apprehensive, wondering if families would go to a movie about bugs. Nicholas sold his heart out and showed a fresh and original idea for a bug movie. The next thing we knew every studio had some form of bug movie in development: *A Bug's Life, Antz, Joe's Apartment, James and the Giant Peach* (which even had a character named Miss Spider in it), and a couple of other bug movies that I can't remember. The irony is that Nicholas's Miss Spider movie, which prompted this whole bug craze, ended up in development hell and never got made. But the point of a lack of originality should not be lost.

The original is always the industry leader. Coke is bigger than Pepsi and Hertz is bigger than Avis. Be an original! The only cautionary words of advice that I have are that people tend to be afraid of newness, and therefore it can be difficult to present a new idea or concept to the market. But don't give up or give in. Because it hasn't been done, people tend to think that it can't be or shouldn't be done. The irony is that once a new product concept is accepted the copycats are not too far behind. Get out your weed whacker and remember, perception is not always reality.

The nice thing about everyone thinking I was crazy for being the first to specialize in the children's entertainment industry is that no one was paying much attention to me (other than a snicker here or there). It was like working in the shade. We had a small amount of success, yet we were not showing up on the radar screens of others. It wasn't until the tremendous success of the *Teletubbies* that a huge spotlight came beaming down on my company and myself. The big question in the industry used to be, Where does he get all this money to promote his brands? And then, the question was, Aren't these properties going to compete with one another? Now all they want to know is, What is he doing next? Every industry has their own set of negativity and questions. You can't allow others to distract you from your goals. It really didn't matter to me what their questions were. The only questions that I was concerned with were, What was the proper marketing plan for the Teletubbies? and What would we do as follow-up to this megahit that we were graced with now that our audience had formed expectations about our company?

My staff reviewed over two thousand shows from around the world (partially because I wanted the next thing to be glorious and partially because offers were flooding in from all points). If I was going to earn my stripes as a *nontraditionalist*, then I had to stick to my mission plan of marketing great stuff for kids in an original fashion. The problem is that the high-quality programming that would satisfy my company's focus was not easy to come by—How often does one see a rainbow or catch a butterfly? Safe*haven* entertainment for children is a mantra I take very seriously, and I was not willing to settle for something good when we were committed to making something great. Safe*haven* entertainment is a perfect combination of focus and nontraditional thinking, because it is clear and concise as well as not the norm in children's programming.

By June of 1998 it became abundantly clear that we (Ragdoll Limited & TibECo) had a huge hit on our hands in the Americas. The Teletubbies had arrived and they arrived big time. It was the biggest preschool television launch in history, thanks to PBS, and the number one toy in the land, thanks to Hasbro. Our rather obscure little company was a part of the second biggest news story of the year (Monica's blue dress was the biggest). It seemed that everything we did was being noticed and companies (and the sheep that ran them) were trying to copy what we were doing. So much for working in the shade. We knew that we were going to have to take doing the unexpected to another extreme while making sure to capitalize on our present platform. While others were focusing on our existing business module of doing things with niche retailers, we decided to pitch them a change up. We had all this unwanted visibility so we decided we might as well use it. My grandmother used to say when God gives you lemons, make lemonade. So instead of being a small (itsy bitsy) company that marketed great stuff for kids, we created a new corporate image. Now, we were going to use the publicity and media exposure to our advantage and present ourselves as a powerhouse full-service entertainment company for children and their caregivers. In actual fact it was more consistent with our goals for global domination anyway. Our first opportunity to do this came in June of 1998 at the International Licensing show at the Javits Center in New York City.

With the licensing industry grossing more than 140 billion dollars, we decided that this was where we were going to do it big. As in years past we were going to spend a majority of our promotional dollars on this show; however this year we had an idea. The brilliant Eileen Potrock, executive director of marketing at TibECo and I schemed up a doozy. We had an idea to establish a variety of sponsorships for the show. Up until now there hadn't been any corporate sponsors for this trade show. In fact, of all the major trade shows that we attend, the International Licensing Show was the only one that did not have any corporate underwriting. With one phone call, Eileen determined that the reason there were no sponsors was not a corporate policy of show management (the new owners of the show), they simply had not gotten around to putting a plan into effect—what a lucky break for us. The trick was that we knew we'd have to buy all of the sponsorships available now and get them grandfathered to us in perpetuity or else the following year the sheep would come grazing. We sat down with the licensing show's management as quickly as possible, and established a variety of sponsorships for the show. Actually, we started by asking them if we could be the exclusive sponsors for the show. They turned that idea down immediately (can't blame a guy for trying). We regrouped and took another approach. We asked for all the individual sponsorships. The show's management believed that they needed to offer the sponsorship opportunities to all of the exhibitors. We knew that no one would buy them because they would be afraid to try something new. So we struck up a deal with the show: They could offer our ideas to the community; however, they could not mention that we were interested in buying any of them. As a result, just as we expected no matter how hard the show's management tried to sell these concepts for further exposure, not one company stepped up to the plate. And as we agreed—TibECo acquired sponsorships for almost 15 different things ranging from the bus routes (with wrapped buses), the stairs, the lanyards, the bags, the tables and napkins in the restaurants, and even the faxes sent by the show's management giving information about the show.

On the first day of the show, our company had such an incredible presence. We immediately, overnight, transformed ourselves into a megalith. All in all it was a perfect day. The other exhibitors were incensed, the attendees were grateful, the show's management was richer (we paid through the nose), and TibECo was well on its way to being a force to be reckoned with. Clearly we were the busiest booth at the show—with both media and customers clamoring to get in to see what we were selling.

It was incredible how successful these sponsorships were for our company's exposure and more important the future success of our brands. The impact of the "show bag" alone had a dramatic effect on the success of a brand. We had decided that the attendee bag for the show would feature the Teletubbies (this would be the only product available other than the Talking Teletubby from Hasbro) and the crowds went wild. Not only did the attendees create a mob scene, but also the exhibitors reeked havoc. This chaos increased manufacturers' and retailers' interest in being a part of the insanity. Our booth was bedlam. And the rest is history.

I remember looking out at the sea of people waiting outside the stanchions of our booth to get an appointment to see us. The other exhibitors were so threatened by our success that they would not allow anyone in their booths who were wearing our lanyards and some went so far as to ask attendees to leave their bags outside as well.

At one point in the show, all I could think of was what's next? What could possibly be next? I looked over at Joan Lambur, then TibECo's general manager of Canada and said, "How are we ever going to top this moment?" And then a little light bulb went on over my head....

Half jokingly, I said to Joan "Its seems like we've mastered this part of the industry. How can we take advantage of it?...I know let's go to Hollywood...I keep reading that they're giving money away to people...making three picture deals." And with that, the die was cast. The fact that neither of us had ever made a movie before didn't stop us. Joan started making cold calls to the studios. And much to our surprise and horror, the studios wanted to meet with us (remember people are sheep) because we had a great success in one medium they wanted to join our conga line. One studio was so overzealous to meet us that they even paid our flights, put us up at the Mondrian Hotel and rented us a fantastic little bright yellow Mercedes convertible (with my fast driving, Joan's hair was never to be the same again).

Joan and I developed a phrase called "the back pocket plan" on this trip. We knew that we had never made a movie and figured that it was only a matter of time until everyone at the studios realized it as well (even the ones that rented us the little bright yellow Mercedes). They were going to realize that this was just one big fat hairy mistake. Once they did, we were sure to be on the next flight back to New York. So Joan developed a "back pocket" plan to meet with the television studios as well.

Ironically, we ended up not needing the back pocket plan, because not only did we do a three-picture deal...we did a FIVE-picture deal with Brad Kevoy's company, MPCA (Motion Picture Corporation of America). Brad was responsible for bringing *Dumb & Dumber* and a number of other successful films to the big screen. They wanted to expand into children's theatricals and use our knowledge of that market, and we wanted to use their knowledge of how to make a feature film.

Because we truly didn't expect anything to materialize in our feature film conversations, Joan frantically had made calls to virtually every children's television executive in Hollywood. Almost despite ourselves, our back pocket plan was able to help us change the face of children's television forever. Despite the fact that many people were not available to meet with us, we did have a few really great meetings. My favorite was a meeting with Sam Ewing, VP International Co-Productions & Acquisitions at Saban International Services. I'll let him tell you about it. Please keep in mind, in my defense, that I had no idea how to pitch a TV show and more important, at that time I had nothing to sell him.

I'd never met Kenn before. I'd met Joan [Lambur]. Joan came in and she brought Kenn. When he came in he was jet-lagged and he brought a basket of croissants. But the basket of croissants was wrapped in linen, the hotel linen. And as it turned out the croissants were from a meeting he was going to have earlier that morning at the hotel which was canceled, and they [Kenn and Joan] had paid a lot of money for hotel crois-

sants and they weren't gonna let them go to waste. They packed them up in the linen that comes with room service and they brought it over here. The linen wasn't bad either. In fact I still have it and I've asked them to just bring another one every time they come by here so I can get a full set.

But generally our first meeting with Kenn was lots of fun. We hit it right off. We both understood what's important in any project and how it should be done, without getting into a lot of talking back and forth about it.

I'm in acquisitions and productions, so I introduced them to Joel Andryc who's in charge of the programming for the kid's area. Actually it's Joel who started talking about It's itsy bitsy Time. *My thing with Kenn and Joan was really about a property. We had a book property on horses and girls—a group of girls, a group of horses, and a series of books. And we have or had the rights to it. I was trying to get some coproduction partners involved in it. Joan's from Canada and I was interested in working with a Canadian company. There had been some previous discussion about that but when Kenn came here we both connected exactly on how the show should be done. For me, that doesn't happen very often. I don't meet many people I connect with right away, who see what the program should be when it gets on the air.*

I was first introduced to the company when I was at the Children's Summit in London. They gave out little books that said The itsy bitsy Entertainment Company. I thought that's a cute name for a company. And then Joan was here and she was Canadian and as I said I do co-productions. She said you've got to meet Kenn and I said great, I'd love to. So that's why they came in. It was real-

ly a hello, how are you, can we talk to see if there's any business to be done? I do a lot of those meetings especially at the markets—MIP, MipCom, NATPE, The Children's Summit in London, anyplace I go. You've got to get out there and meet them and greet them. It was really rare to feel that click. Kenn's got a great sense of humor; he's got an unusual twist on things. One of the things I appreciated about Kenn and his croissants was in the story. Because it was like it came from A Hotel Room. I've been a producer for over 30 years, and Kenn's a marketer. The main thing you want to do is get people's attention whether you're producing or you're marketing. You want to get people's attention right off the bat, and he got my attention right off the bat, because it was a funny way of doing it. He was really open.

It didn't appear contrived and that's one of the reasons why I like him. He's often spur of the moment and quickly he gets the picture. He sees the picture of the way it's supposed to be. Kenn's got so much energy and he's thinking all the time. If you're in the same zone with him, he sparks your ideas of things that are possible. He may not have the answer right there. You know a salesperson might come in, or a producer, to pitch something and you know the sales pitch. It's rare that you meet someone that gets your own mind working adding to the possibilities as to how we could do this. Kenn's one of those rare people that has that ability to get other people to start thinking of possibilities. I don't know how better to define that. So when he started talking and exploring and what not, I'm sure when he had this meeting with Joel and Joel probably said hey you know, here, here's how we could actually put this all together.

We understood from meeting with Sam, his boss Joel Andryc (a really nice guy who put up with a great deal to ultimately become our true believer) and ultimately Hiam Saban (one of my inspirations) that they needed to have a big preschool hit. Joel can take it from here....

It was about the same time that Teletubbies had hit. Kenn was really riding a big wave of success and excitement with the company growing so rapidly. And he had an air of confidence about himself, but also displayed a real knowledge of the kids arena. He seemed to have a real sense on the marketplace and what worked and didn't work. Which then got me interested in trying to do business with someone that has had one hit under his belt and perhaps bring us something that would put the Fox Family Channel on the map. At the time we had just gotten into a lot of the programming that hadn't even launched Fox Family Channel yet. So we were out trying to figure out what we were going to do for the first year of the Fox Family Channel. What was going to work what was not going work, and so it was the right time for us, too.

It was very much more of an informal meeting. It was I think more of a greet and meet. I think at the time they had met Sam Ewing and Sam then had introduced them to me, knowing my programming needs and that Kenn had a couple of different ideas, but it was not an official pitch. It was more of an opportunity for me to get to know Kenn and for Kenn to get to know me and listen to what my needs were, and what our plans were for Fox Family.

At that time we had a block of programming starting to come together, but we were trying to create a real environ-

ment for the preschool block. So much of it is to create a safe haven so that the parents or the caregiver knows this is quality programming. We had penciled in Captain Kangaroo *and* Mr. Moose's Fun Times, *which was a character from Captain Kangaroo. Mr. Moose hosted a half hour of short interstitials, which was similar to what* It's itsy bitsy Time! [IibT!] *is all about. So we were thinking along the same lines that there is a lot of great quality programming out there. How do you market and brand it, and package it? I thought after meeting with Kenn that he had some really great ideas and that he was probably one of the right people to be in business with in order to make our mark in preschool. He was also looking at the environment. It is very competitive out there. You have Nickelodeon, just at the time* Blues Clues *was hitting with high ratings, and the toys were coming out. You had* Bear in the Blue House, *you had all the PBS programming, so during the daytime the preschool programming to capture those eyeballs, it's real competitive.*

At the first meeting we did not even talk about IibT! I think there was a subsequent meeting and Kenn had come back then and said, "Hey I have vision of something real interesting. To create a block that is completely delivered to you that would be a great vehicle for marketing and promotion. That has it all together. It was almost a turnkey operation." I had 12 hours of programming a day, 7 days a week to launch. So this was like turning off the light switch one day from the old Family Channel and the next morning turning it back onto something completely new. This was the first time that an entire network had been reprogrammed from start to finish overnight. Usually when a network builds, there are two ways. With the traditional network, they will build day by day or night by night. And then roll out like Fox did or UPN's doing or the WB. Cable networks, when they launch, they don't launch in 75 million homes, 100 percent cable penetration overnight. They might launch in 2 million and then grow to 4 and then grow to 16. And here we were, we had the opportunity to relaunch ourselves in 75 million homes because we bought the old Family Channel.

Kenn came in and said I can help you in preschool, I know what I'm doing. And he has everything to back himself up. He worked with Britt Allcroft, launching a very successful franchise, and then with his company the Teletubbies, *which at the time was number one. A lot of the ideas that he had made a lot of sense. There were two components to taking the leap of faith with Kenn. One was his ability to sell us on the creative, like I mentioned before, his expertise in the preschool in the market in the past and the different franchises that he has been involved with. His vision for what he wanted for his brand and how to market it and some of the shows that he was going to bring to the table. So that was more of the creative and the programming and we felt that he could deliver that. On the other end too, there was a financial incentive with Hasbro.*

It's very difficult to find or to make money in the preschool arena. Traditionally toy companies and advertisers don't normally advertise in this day part because the younger kids do not make decisions. They do not make buying choices. It is the parents that buy for the preschool audience. And so a lot of the advertisers stay out of preschool. What Kenn was able to do was to bring Hasbro in as a corporate sponsor, much like what PBS does with a lot of their programming. And so that also made a lot of sense for use from a business point of view. Kenn not only has the creative contacts to deliver a great show that will get us ratings but he also has the business contacts to bring in advertisers and sponsors. I think this is a unique situation with preschool. The way that you make money on preschool programming is at the back end, the merchandising and the licensing. Everything from PBS shows like Sesame Street, *it's the merchandising and licensing. It's the Sesame Street Stores. It's the apparel; it's the toys.* Blues Clues *is the same thing,* Teletubbies, Bear in the Blue House. *All of these shows are not making a profit from the programming. Where the money comes from is selling the merchandising and the licensing. So in order to succeed, bring a sponsor and have programming that could somehow be successful and have a merchandising and licensing campaign. And then it works from a business point of view.*

Once we agreed to work with Fox Family Channel, the big question was, what were we going to air with them and how were we going to get it produced?

I was feeling a little pressure. I kept thinking, never let them see you sweat. Somehow we would make it happen. My first question was, what would my father do? Ultimately I knew that he would advise me to think of the customer. Who were they and what were their needs? The trick was I had to understand the difference between their needs and their wants. You have to give them what they need and it would be nice to then give them what they want.

In this case we knew that we had three different customers here: the network, the caregiver, and ultimately the child. In the case of the network, we knew that they needed a really good television series for young children. So we took it one step at a time. We set out to find/produce the best of the best. This series would possibly be the programming that helped define the image and importance of this relatively new network, much in the same way that *Sesame Street* helped define PBS.

We knew from previous experience that the caregiver was concerned with the safety of the programming. Would the shows have gratuitous violence and aggressive behavior? Would there be sexual innuendo? And what outside influences would the television commercials bring? From talking to hundreds of parents and caregivers we learned that they used television in three different ways for their children—as a caregiver, as a treat, and as an educator. Any series that we were going to create was going to have to take all of these ideas into consideration. The time of day was also very important so the caregiver could fit it into their schedule. Different times of day could potentially have different programming requirements.

The important lesson for us to understand was that every new venture that we aligned ourselves to would have different concerns and questions that would need to be addressed prior to being able to meet our goals of making great stuff for kids. No matter what type of business a person runs or product a person makes, with each new enterprise they need to identify their concerns and get the appropriate answers with regards to meeting their goals.

Insight Into Your Audience

For the child, we knew that the series above all else, was going to be funny. Fun was fine but funny was essential. You use humor to engage the child and once they are engaged you can embrace and/or teach them. We knew the importance of repetition for children and knew that the series had to air daily. Also we needed to keep in mind that children have limited attention spans. The concept of a 30-minute story line is too long and is not really ideal for a preschool child.

The most difficult step was finding content that matched our goals: After several months of searching the globe, we found a few gems. These animated children's shows were created, produced, and equally important funded in Europe. There was an overabundance of great programming for preschoolers in Europe with truly extraordinary production values. The big problem was that the majority of these shows have a running time of less than 10 minutes, which will not fit the standard North American television format. Because they are not half-hour or hour shows, the stations don't have the ability to fit them into their programming. Now for the dilemma (and TibECo's opportunity), the particular shows we found ranged from 1 minute to 10 minutes in length. The shows were too special on their own and the length of the shows was perfect for preschoolers' attention spans. How were we going to make them work on U.S. television?

One increasingly common solution to these "odd-length" programs is to produce a show around the animation—what's referred to as a "wraparound." Such was the success of *ShiningTime Station* for *Thomas the Tank Engine* or *The Noddy Shoppe* for *Noddy*. Although this formula had worked in the past, it was clearly not going to work for this project. The thing is that these gems were all different sizes and lengths and the cost of producing enough quantity to satisfy our needs would have been wildly unaffordable (more than $25,000,000). An idea starting brewing in my mind, but would we be able to pull it off?

What if we took these shows and created a variety hour for kids? It wasn't a new idea, yet there was a way to make a variation of a classic concept from my childhood television memories. Immediately we liked the idea. We knew that caregivers could feel comfortable with this safe and fun format. We thought about what shows the parents of today grew up watching. In a very quick minute, Joan and I started playing around with developing a show called *It's itsy bitsy Time* (sung to the Howdy Doody theme song). I had my attorneys go to the copyright offices and bought the rights to use the song for about $20. Things were starting to come together. Our gems had a new home! The four core programs—*The*

Animal Shelf, Tom and Vicky, Charlie & Mimmo, and *64 Zoo Lane*
were the anchor shows that would make up the first season of this
block of time on the Fox Family Channel. We were so close; I just
wasn't sure how to make the shows link up.

There are no rules as to what makes nontraditional thinking
other than not to take anything for granted. We have another
expression in our company that says make choices, not decisions. A
choice requires that the person look at all the alternatives and
options available to him or her, whereas a decision does not. Joan
and I knew our goals and now we needed to creatively look at all of
the options available to us to make them happen.

Because of the costs of producing a series, we wanted to make
something that was as classic in look as possible. We did not want to
have to redo this series in a couple of years. And we needed a brand-
ed look that did not detract or favor any one individual segment. I
was not interested in having a presenter introduce the series within
the series, because it would take the children out of the magic and
then we'd have to get their attention all over again each time we
went back into the episodic part of the program. I also needed the
segues to be travelable because of both the cost and time to produce
new material, and we knew that once the show was a hit then pro-
grammers from around the world would want to buy our format.
Once we had a list of all the criteria, it was just a matter of time.

Eventually, we developed a circus theme and created a magical
man and fantastic circus tent that appears in between every component of the series and brings the audience to the next segment without ever breaking the connection with the child. We had it all figured out except for one thing. This show was being created for commercial television, not PBS (the established outlet for caregivers of
preschoolers), what were we going to do about the commercials?

The caregivers that we spoke to all stressed how comfortable they
felt about PBS programming and a big reason was that it was one of
the only commercial-free environment for their kids on television.
We knew that parents and caregivers felt uncomfortable with children's programs that have commercials, but networks were in the

business of selling commercial time. In order to create a safe*haven* program, we needed to deliver not only great programming, but also great commercial-free programming. I could have sold this series to PBS and have created something else for Fox Family Channel. The problem was that I already had three series on air with PBS and was talking to them about two more. Eventually I was going to compete with myself for airtime and I needed to expand my relationships with other networks. My grandmother always said to me that it wasn't smart to have all of my eggs in one basket. No problem…now all we had to do was make Fox Family Channel commercial free.

The idea of making commercial-free programming on a commercial network was enough to make a nonbeliever get up, dust himself off, and go home. And yet Joan and I were in for a penny, in for a pound. We knew that there was a way to make it happen. Eventually, we realized that we could find a network the same revenue from one source as they were going to collect from a variety of partners. We were determined to find them an underwriter.

After several years in the licensing industry, I had a very strong relationship with Hasbro. I went to them with a concept of putting together a sponsorship package for *It's itsy bitsy Time!*, It was a good idea for both of us. Hasbro could potentially reach millions of parents and caregivers with a specific soft-sell branding message for their company, parents would feel safer, children would get great programming, and we would get our block on television. The key to every deal that I get involved with is that everyone always wins. Although it seemed simple enough, apparently it was a radical idea. We were so focused in our goals that although our behavior seemed normal to us it was in fact not traditional for everyone else around us.

In actual fact we went to a huge multibillion dollar company and suggested that they spend money to promote their brand without making a specific product endorsement on a commercial network that was going to run commercially uninterrupted programming for their children's block. In hindsight I guess it was a rather farfetched plan. Part of being focused and a true believer is that often you don't realize how unrealistic your dreams are until you've achieved them.

Joan and I suggested that *It's itsy bitsy Time brought to you by Hasbro* could be like the *Mobil Masterpiece Theatre* or like the old *Texaco Hour*. In record time, they got the concept and understood the overall value it could provide for their company (thank you Alan, Herb, and Willa). Our partners at Hasbro were willing to share in our vision and be associated with a new innovative program that would offer great quality entertainment and learning experiences for the youngest of children. Hopefully for them their wonderfully simple message will generate a great deal of goodwill for them.

For years, the FCC has been trying to get commercial-free programming for children on commercial networks, to no avail. And then everything changes, because in walks two nontraditional-thinking dodos from a rather obscure little company. It wasn't until after the deal was done that Joan and I realized the magnitude of what we had achieved. I'm not sure that I would have had the nerve to try this project if I had known the scope of it in advance. Such risk taking is certainly an element of nontraditional thinking. Because as a nontraditionalist you are often traveling into unchartered territory, often, you are taking risks. The rewards of successfully establishing something new whether it is a new distribution channel or a new product to market, far outweigh the risks taken to achieve them. What's a little egg on your face, if you have the chance to change the future—even if in just some small way.

And with Hasbro's financial commitment, *It's itsy bitsy Time!* a commercially uninterrupted program was born. I only wish it were as simple as it looks here on paper. I remember how difficult it was to sign the agreement.

We wanted to take advantage of the exposure of MIP-TV (a huge television event in the south of France—where all eyes on the entertainment industry are focused) to sign our agreement with Fox Family Channel and our company. The negotiations actually came down to the wire with conference calls between New York, Los Angeles, Toronto, and Bologna (where I was at the time for a book fair). Between the time zone differences I was virtually up around the clock for almost 3 straight days. In fact, for 21 straight days leading up to MIP I didn't sleep more than 3 or 4 hours a day. With a great deal of determination and luck (strategy + opportunity = luck), the deal was signed and we were able to get our press release out in time for MIP. Timing is often an important element in success (if you do not get your product out in time, then someone can get there ahead of you—damn sheep!). Timing is quintessential for publicity and publicity is quintessential for a small company. We had a great deal of stories in the press, but much more important, we were the talk of the fair. Huge companies were approaching us, congratulating us, and trying to find ways to work with us. Both Joan's and my dance cards were full that show. All in, we had almost 100 meetings in 4.5 days.

One of the more challenging aspects of "thinking out of the box" is getting your partners to share your newfound thinking. Hopefully you've chosen "believers" to partner with, which is the first step. Thinking "nontraditionally" is really important in today's highly competitive world. A key advantage of a small company is its ability to take risks and take them quickly. Often big companies get bogged down in politics. If you have to work with a company that is political in nature, my only advice is to be relentless and not back down. You will be amazed at how far your will and belief can take you.

When we launched the Teletubbies toys and videos, we had to deal with two highly political organizations, and we had to convince them to take a very radical approach to selling a product.

Teletubbies launched on PBS April 16, 1998. There was a great deal of buildup to the launch of the show, with its success in the United Kingdom and an extensive promotional teaser campaign (thanks again to PBS and the media). Needless to say, our licensing partners were true believers in the *Teletubbies*. They were also commercially minded companies whose reason for getting involved with *Teletubbies* also included making monies. So when I told Hasbro and Warner Home Video (PBS Kids distributors) that I wanted to launch the Talking Teletubbies and home videos exclusively to the specialty channels, you can imagine their reaction.

We knew that launching Hasbro's Talking Teletubbies in limited release was the right decision. However, our partners thought that this strategy would potentially put them into a difficult situation with their other retail relationships. For us there was no compromise—not only was it an incredible publicity opportunity but it was essential to building the demand for the toys, controlling the sales, and most important making sure that children responded favorably to the toys. We had an additional concern as we got closer to the product's launch date that perhaps Hasbro had not made enough of the toys to satisfy demand (who could have predicted the demand 9 months ahead of time). We thought that it was better to not put a retailer into business until we knew that we could keep them in business. It's one thing to not have the customers in the first place than to have them and not be able to keep them. As a result, we were forced to limit the channels of distribution of the product and required Hasbro to do a slow roll out. As more product became available, we rolled out the products to broader channels.

The situation with Warner Brothers was very similar. The difference was that this was simply not something that was done in the video industry. Street date is street date (the date a video could be sold at retail). No if's, and's or but's about it. They were concerned about how larger video retailers were going to react to our selling six specialty retailers the product a few weeks in advance of street date. It is considered a no-no to break street date for a product. Michelle Kanter, Director of video and publishing, and I had to make a very difficult decision. We knew all of the facts and yet we believed that the information we could garner would potentially be invaluable. The plan called for us to sell two titles on the initial release. Was two the right number? Would they sell evenly? Was the price too high? Too low? We simply needed to gather sales information. We looked at the facts and then made a choice, not a decision, and broke street date for the six specialty store retailers.

From the initial orders it was clear that the large retailers were buying the goods evenly and yet we suspected that the consumer was going to favor one title over the other. In the test we discovered that although both were excellent, one video was in fact clearly stronger than the other. This information became vital from our company's perspective and did direct the future marketing plans for the brand. As an example, as a result of the initial launch, we put out only one title at a time now.

Both of these partners were frustrated by our determination to do things differently, at first. However once each of their products hit number one on their respective charts, new ideas became much more rapidly accepted. It is funny how the perception of being a mad man can be changed to a genius when you become successful.

I must make a statement for the record that being stubborn is not the same thing as being determined. Make sure you understand your motivation. Being a good partner is as important as any part of the process. To put your foot down without listening to the needs of your partner is not effective partnership. If we were going to think nontraditionally and then act nontraditionally, then we needed to make ourselves accountable for our actions. Part of being a true believer is taking your lumps with your sugar. In the case of Warner Brothers video releases, Michelle told Warner that if they received any hostile calls from retailers that she would be willing to take complete responsibility for the early shipping decision. This took the pressure off of Warner and kept our relationship intact.

To be a nontraditionalist you also have to have a strong backbone. You must be determined, *but* you must listen to the outside influences. Pick your battles, and don't give in until you are convinced that what someone else is suggesting is better than what you are suggesting. It is important that no matter what your idea is it must be a win-win for you and whoever is affected by it. Self-righteousness or indignation will cost you more in the long term than it is worth in the short term.

Whether you are the owner of a small company or an employee in a big company, you must remember that just because something has worked for you in the past does not mean that it will be the best choice for you in every instance. Remember that the only rule to becoming a nontraditionalist is that there are no rules. A really bright man told me recently that no two situations are ever exactly the same, similar maybe but never the same.

It is important that you truly believe in your work and that you can communicate your vision effectively to others thereby helping to motivate them to follow your goals. You need to keep your eyes and mind open to new ideas and new ways of looking at the box, whether they come from the small company, the large company, *a lowly employee* or the lady who sells you the coffee in the morning. And a great idea is a great idea!

When completing this workshop, it's important to keep in mind that the route you take will be very different from the route you took to look at your focus. In order to build your foundation, your focus, you are looking at a straight line. To build a nontraditional wall you need to think of your line as a maze. You need to be relentless in finding your solution because you may hit a lot of dead ends before you reach your goal.

Answer these questions to build the third wall of your house.

1. What is your challenge?
2. What are three solutions for dealing with your challenge?
3. Look at your three solutions; pick one and develop a solution.
4. Take that solution and talk it over with someone who is close to your challenge.

Use that person's input to create your new solution.

Who Is the End User?

When in Rome...sell pasta.

Who is your audience? How can you serve them better? Those are two of the most relevant questions that any business can and should be constantly asking themselves.

As many companies start becoming successful, they lose sight of their initial objective. Sometimes it's because of the money or the possibility of immediate gratification, but usually it is because they forget about their audience—the very people who made them successful in the first place. There are dozens of examples of mass retailers going out of business because they wanted to "upgrade their customer." What was wrong with their original customer—why couldn't they just expand from their base? PBS added *Barney* (in order to broaden the socioeconomics of their audience) and the *Teletubbies* (in order to broaden the age of their audience) to their schedule in order to maintain their existing base and to expand upon in it.

The single most important philosophy we used in the building of The itsy bitsy Entertainment Company is that the end user was and always will be our focus. In our case, the end user is the almighty preschooler. We at TibECo are faced with an unusual problem. Unlike most end users, it is not appropriate to market your products directly to our specific target audience. Because our audience is so young, we need to reach our intended target by reaching out to their caregivers. As a result we have to focus on both the safety and the "playability" of our brand to achieve the acceptance of this very narrow group necessary to sustain the company and allow its future growth. As a result of the dual audience that we serve, it seemed that the more control we could have in the process the better our chances of answering everyone's needs.

It was always my intention to have TibECo become a full-fledged entertainment company and as vertically integrated as possible. I knew, however, that the point of least resistance for the entertainment industry would be for me to reenter the market in the capacity for which I was already known. I had been very fortunate to work with Britt Alcroft (the person and the company) on *Thomas the Tank Engine*. And I was very closely associated with Thomas's success off the television screen. I thought that people would welcome me back in a role that felt similar to the one where they last knew me (sort of like typecasting an actor). Perception is not always reality.

The Power of the Misconception

I was not as welcomed back as I had expected. Many thought that I was a one hit wonder and the concept of specializing within the field of licensing was unheard of. The naysayers kept telling me that I was crazy. The "experts" said that specializing in preschool entertainment just wouldn't be a profitable business, and that I was destined to fail. One so-called expert went so far as to say that I was about to commit professional suicide. Others suggested that property owners would not give me their properties for fear that I would be competing with myself. I, on the other hand, thought if TibECo developed a series of marketing plans for a variety of preschool properties, then everyone would win. By the mere fact that we knew what each property was going to do, we would in fact be able to guarantee that the properties would not be in competition with each other. If they did not join us, then we would have no choice but to compete with them. I held strong. My thought was that if someone wanted heart surgery they would go to a heart surgeon and not a general practitioner. If a great creator wanted to be represented by an agent (I hate that terminology), then they would want an agent that knew the intimacies of their business. I learned from the garment center, early on, that children's clothes are *not* the same as adult clothes, just smaller (but that is another story) and neither is their entertainment.

All the statistics were there and yet no one seemed to be reading them. Children were leaving traditional entertainment at a much earlier age than in recent years. Basic game sales were down and yet preschool was starting to uptrend. Grandparents were living longer with greater disposable income. Parents were starting to take a more proactive role in helping select their children's entertainment vehicles. And yet the market was not being responsive to the changes in the marketplace. There was a misconception—a commonly held belief that something was one thing when in fact it was something else. Part of our success in building TibECo was that we were able to identify this "market misconception" and capitalize on it.

Understanding the nuances of your marketplace is key when you are the little guy or if you have limited funds to promote/launch a new product. You do not want to waste any funds or spend monies on a segment of the market that is not likely to purchase your product.

Television advertisers believed that preschool-aged children had no disposable income and therefore were not a group worth advertising to. I believed at the time, and have now found to be true, that TV advertisers were creating a self-fulfilling prophecy. In fact the very youngest children control a majority of the family's disposable income (as much as 75 cents of every dollar). Virtually every decision being made by the parents of preschoolers reflected the needs or wants of the preschooler. They go to restaurants to satisfy their youngest children, they buy homes in neighborhoods that have the best school systems for their child, they buy cars that consider the safety of their children, and buy more home videos for their children than for themselves. Even their vacation selection considers the youngest child. If you don't believe the influence of today's preschooler on the family then you don't have a preschooler. I can invite you all to my brother and sister-in-law's house and you can watch one in action. The thought was if they can't speak then they can't ask for what they want. Tsk, tsk, tsk.

Often, the misconception is such a widely held belief that it takes nontraditional thinking to breakthrough. Certainly that was the case with my company specializing in a field that was perceived to be of limited value. The challenge here was to find ways of communicating to third parties that their beliefs were incorrect. Above all we had to show potential partners that they were not looking at the whole picture. All the facts were there, just no one had put them all together, until we came along.

In my career, I have seen firsthand the impact of the preschooler at retail. The preschool business has exploded. *Sesame Street* alone has been reported to have generated more than $10,000,000,000 in sales. Not to mention other huge projects like *The Cabbage Patch Kids, Arthur, Barney,* and of course my personal favorite...the *Teletubbies.*

In working within my company and with our partners, it is important that everyone look beyond their typical response to business decisions and consider whether this would make children smile, because they are our audience. It is truly imperative to understand your end user's needs and wants in order to make sure that you are creating a satisfied customer. Remember a satisfied customer is a repeat customer.

I should interrupt myself here to tell you that there are two types of greed—short-term greed (the greed of amateurs) and long-term greed (the big kahuna). I make no apologies for being a for-profit company. As I said before, I believe that a company can truly make great stuff for children and make a whole lot of money at the same time. This can be the best solution as long as the principal group does not loose sight of its original goal and its audience.

Understand the Terrain

Imagine, if you would, a little company with all of a dozen people working in it managed by a guy who never took a business course sitting down with a multibillion-dollar public giant of a company with hundreds of MBA's to discuss business strategy. As hard as it is to believe, that is our relationship with Hasbro—the toy giant. This process started with the introduction of the Talking Teletubbies— the first toy to be created for the Hasbro Teletubby line.

If we had rolled out the product range quickly, it would have made tens of millions of dollars for everyone. However, we had bigger goals, and I had a promise to keep (Anne had asked me to expose her series to as many children as possible—purely with the hope of making a child's world a little bit happier). I, on the other hand, wanted it all. Global domination means not settling for a piece of the pie, when you can have the whole thing with ice cream on top. Whoever said you can't have everything never achieved global domination and never will.

I wanted to create a high-quality long-term best-selling brand for children and the caregivers in their lives. I wanted to build the reputation and success of the series on the screen *before* we exploited the series off the screen, as a means of winning the respect of the caregiver and the love of the child.

We worked very closely with Hasbro to develop a slow and deliberate role out for this toy. We needed to be sure that the product was right, that children would be happy, and that their caregivers would be able to find a steady supply of a product they approved of on the retailers' shelves. I was not interested in getting a product to market quickly if it did not have the play pattern that a child would recognize or if it was not offered at a price that parents would find acceptable. One of the things that was difficult for Hasbro to understand was that we were not interested in being the cheapest product in the market. The Talking Barney toy was selling in Wal-Mart and Toys "R" Us for anywhere from $17.99 to $19.99, and I wanted our toy to have a suggested retail of $29.99, as long as it had a perceived value of at least $29.99. I am very proud that this toy became the best-selling featured plush toy for 1998; however I am more excited that it goes down in the history books as one of the most profitable toys of all time at retail as well. Clearly, it was a win-win situation for all involved. Additionally, not only were the Talking Teletubbies number one so were their woodboard puzzles, their rotational molded figures, and several other categories of toys and ancillary products.

We always strive to develop products that stay true to the essence of the property. In order to do this, we spend a great deal of time learning and understanding what elements of our projects the child is responding to and then, only after we discover a true understanding, we try to create products that express those elements. I think our greatest strength in the product arena is that we keep asking questions both of our audience as well as our manufacturing partners. Sometimes we ask so we can learn more about that company's specific manufacturing process; however, usually we are trying to get them to make a safer and more novel product.

Again, The itsy bitsy Entertainment Company is unusual with regards to its target audience. In addition to our direct consumer we have the additional responsibility to create safe*haven* entertainment™ both on and off of the screen and to satisfy the concerns of their caregivers as well. We would never develop or provide any form of entertainment that had gratuitous violence or sexually explicit material, regardless of whether the child liked it or not—the parent/caregiver would never approve. In order to stay true to our mission, we need to achieve a feeling of acceptance by the parents and caregivers *and* make the children smile.

All of the products, advertising, and promotion that we do are an extension of the child's viewing experience. We often test possible

products with young children across the countr
them to go to market. We recognize that we are
for children in a rapidly changing technological env..
that as a result their world as well as ours is constantly changing—
we therefore need to look at products all the time to make sure that
we are staying current with the environment. We want our view-
ers/customers to know that they can trust us to provide them with
wholesome loving products that are a responsible reflection of our
time. As mentioned earlier, the hardest thing is managing the
expectations of others, because it takes constant updating. With
preschoolers or any other target audience, you want your consumer
to know what they can expect and that there is a commitment from
you to ensure that their expectations will be met.

Focused Doesn't Mean Limited

A key secret here is that just because you are focused in one market
segmentation doesn't mean that you can or should make only one
product. Just because you make potholders does not mean that you
can't make the pots as well. The itsy bitsy Entertainment Company is
a broad-based entertainment company with a narrow focus. Our company's motto is "To be free to learn, Children must be free to dream!"
This philosophy is a constant in our business choices because we
think of it as "a broadening" and not "a limiting." In the past 5 years
we have opened divisions that deal with domestic licensing, domestic
television sales, worldwide television production, feature films, international television and merchandising, and television relations. We
have even established a consumer products division. If it is entertainment for children, whether it is on the screen or on the shelves, we
ask ourselves two very simple little questions (we refer to them in the
company as the "itsy bitsy questions"): Will this allow a parent to feel
that their child is safe? Will it make a child smile?

Sometimes, when dealing with issues of the "long-termness" of
the brands we market, we have to make business choices that will

limit our short-term income. Limiting your efforts to a specific target audience can limit immediate cash potential in preparation for long-term rewards. Although there were many stories over the past 5 years, about how we work with different companies to focus on our target audience, there are a few which stand out as clearly as a story about S. Goldberg.

It is truly critical in the development of a long-term brand not to allow the wolf in sheep's clothing get into your barn. One of our licensees, S. Goldberg, the largest domestic slipper manufacturer in America, was having a tremendous success in producing slippers based on one of our series. This preschool brand was the most successful in their company's 100 years of doing business. Like all phenomena, the demand for the shoes was greater than expected. The interesting thing was that older children, teens, and adults also wanted shoes for themselves based on this preschool series. My dear friend Bernie Leifer (who will probably not speak to me again after he reads this) ran the company, kept coming back to us to ask for the right to produce adult slippers. At the time, we restricted Bernie from selling anything larger than toddler size, and he thought it was a great idea to provide the adult fans of the series a chance to have their own slippers. He became increasingly frustrated inasmuch as he was forced to turn down orders from his customers, because we would not allow him to take advantage of these incremental sales (which would have added up to millions and millions of dollars in additional sales). Of course, we liked the idea of making more monies, but this violated our number one rule of staying true to our audience. We believed that creating products for adults based on this series only diluted the fact that the series was special for the little ones—like a private club. Once you let adults in you take the specialness away for the child. Does Bernie really care? Does it matter? He is obligated to make as much money for his company and I am obligated to do for mine. Although it appeared to be a way to extend our brand, the potential repercussion outweighed the advantages. We were concerned about the brand looking like a fad or a trend in the market; we were going for gold—a long-term classic. Ultimately the possibility that this brand dilution could affect our long-term relationship with children made it impossible for us to grant additional rights or to extend the sizes of his footwear. Remember a little forever is always better than a lot for once.

Another interesting situation developed when we decided to do third-party promotions for the Teletubbies. The first QSR (quick-service restaurant) promotional partner we chose to work with was Burger King. We planned a promotion with them for spring 1999; a full year after the series went on air. This was the first time that Burger King had ever worked with a target age as young as Teletubbies. And of equal importance, it was the first time that a PBS series was going to be a part of a national promotion of this sort. Richard Taylor, senior vice president of marketing of Burger King, is probably the best person to talk about Burger King's expectations and how we worked to fulfill and surpass them....

It was really the first time that we focused on such a young audience. If you look at the actual target for this particular property, it basically skews from not much older than birth to just a few years old and that was a departure for us. When we entered into this agreement with Kenn, we realized that this was an unusual promotion. We negotiated different deal terms. In fact, this thing was done quite hurriedly in a conference room at Atlanta Hartsfield Airport where we all flew in just to meet because our schedules were all at odds with one another. We sat down and hammered out the entire agreement and really the last thing that we ever discussed was the financial model of how we were going to make this thing work. What we talked about was quite refreshing for me. We talked about "What is good for kids?" and "Is there a message to give to their caregivers?" "Let's talk about nutritional information that can go on tray liners." "Let's make sure here that we offer things that aren't available anywhere else." "Let's do things that have never been done in the QSR category before." And so we created Tubby Custard. We talked about all the different ways that we would speak to caregivers and to kids about this promotion. And we did a lot of innovative things that just hadn't been tried before.

From our prospective in terms of giving our consumers what they expect from Burger King we must identify the right property. Without a doubt Teletubbies was it. It was not only a very positive thing for kids and a positive learning experience but it also offered that fun and excitement and collectability that kids absolutely need to have in toys. We're pretty much ruled by kids and they don't want to go to Burger King and have an educational experience. It is supposed to be fun for them and so if we can slip education in and give them something of value, that gives us a real feel good.

Teletubbies was a very successful promotion. We were very pleased with the volume of kids meals that were delivered to kids. And that is a real good indicator for us that the children are embracing the program that we've put together. And the performance was very, very positive. However, it wasn't without its ups and downs. Tubby Custard, in retrospect, didn't work well for us. And as we look back on it, one of the learning points was that parents didn't know what Tubby Custard was. We advertised the name but custard is not a word that translates well in the United States. Kids in the United Kingdom know exactly what custard is but kids in America hear custard and they think it sounds bad. If we had told them it was Jello-brand vanilla pudding, we would have blown the doors off. Itsy Bitsy and Ragdoll did not want us to identify vanilla pudding, and frankly that is something that we should have done. Everything else was extremely positive. And I think it was fun to bring something new to this particular category. I think the Teletubbies really rocked people and I think the entire QSR category was rather surprised.

My friendship with Kenn has been one of the more enjoyable relationships that I've had over the years. I've been lucky to meet a lot of great people but it was very interesting working with Kenn, who had such a long-term vision of where he wanted this property to go. And at the same time, it was a pleasure to have someone who was much more motivated by the message to kids as opposed to the bottom line in terms of dollars. I think he lives by the credo that you should do what you love and the money follows. Or maybe I'd just say that nice guys can finish first.

For TibECo, there are several questions that need to be explored before we agree to take on a new project. We evaluate potential broadcast content by asking these questions:

1. Will it make a child smile?
2. Does it ask the question, "Is anything possible?"
3. Does it have a great story? (Most people don't realize that the reason most book-based projects for preschoolers are effective is because they tell great stories.)
4. Is it unique? Does it have a reason for being?
5. Does the material speak to the child in a way that builds confidence?
6. Is the content appropriate for a preschooler? (Let's face it—a lot of the material that is available to children is truly inappropriate and the line seems to be blurring for many in Hollywood

each day. Unfortunately, everyday life exposes children to enough awful stuff that we should be trying to find the good things to help nurture their growth. So for us, content must be nonviolent, noncompetitive, nonaggressive, and nonsexual.

7. Is the material presented in a way that celebrates the similarities between people, not the differences?
8. Will parents or caregivers believe that the environment is safe for their child?
9. Do we feel passionate about it?

We create offscreen entertainment by asking similar questions:

1. Is it huggable? Does it make children smile?
2. Does it have a reason for being/is it unique?
3. Will the _____ help build a child's confidence?
4. Is the _____ appropriate for a preschooler? (You wouldn't believe some of the products companies have approached us to produce—including chocolate Easter bunnies filled with RUM!)
5. Is the material presented in a way that celebrates the similarities between people, not the differences? Is it noncompetitive? (One way we follow this philosophy is that all of the board games we create have common goals; thus everyone wins and there are no losers.)
6. Will parents or caregivers feel completely comfortable with the environment for their child?
7. Is there a perceived value?
8. Do we feel passionate about this product?

With the entertainment we market, we keep one thing in mind—our end user. We've passed on thousands of potential opportunities because they don't fit our definition of great preschool entertainment or the needs of our end user. Whether they have the potential to become a moderate success is of no importance to me, because ultimately it dilutes our company's brand equity or goodwill with our audience.

Even the best-laid plans cannot guarantee a success. I have a very unfortunate example. *Tots TV* is a magnificent bilingual preschool show about celebrating the similarities in children created by Anne Wood and Ragdoll Productions that began airing on PBS October 6, 1996. The show got an extraordinary response being picked up by nearly 285 of the 340 PBS affiliates in its first 3 months of broadcast, obviously indicating a very high demand for the series. The characters were cute and their messages were empowering to kids. The other way this show is different is that one of the characters speaks only Spanish, making *Tots TV* the only truly bilingual preschool series on television in America. By early 1997, the merchandise was ready—we had dolls, a variety of other toys, clothing, accessories, videos, and a book deal lined up.

Even though we had a show that children loved and a solid reputation for marketing hits, it was not catching on with retailers or manufacturers. So what went wrong? Funny you should ask.

PBS had a show about ethnic diversity on their airwaves that was funded by the Corporation for Public Broadcasting (CPB). This show called *Puzzle Place* taught children the concept of celebrating the differences in others: a concept I find much too adultlike for children to follow. Unfortunately, *Puzzle Place* bombed at retail (and I mean bombed). Well since it was a show about ethnic diversity and *Tots TV* was a show perceived to be about ethnic diversity....Need I say more? Just remember that perception is not always reality. Eventually, we let our American book partner out of their rather lucrative deal (and substantial advance) and turned our attention globally to territories where *Puzzle Place* was not being sold. Why beat a dead horse? American retailers for the time being had made up their minds. The fact that *Tots TV* was a huge hit in the United Kingdom was of little consequence to the licensing community in America. No matter how much work you put into the launch of a new product, you cannot control outside factors. The key is to not be too rigid in your planning. Look at the outside influences and adapt to them. As a little side note, if *Puzzle*

Place had been a huge retail success, then (because people are sheep) *Tots TV* would also have been a big hit ("Get me one of those shows on ethnic diversity").

We knew we had a great product and that our challenge was to find an unbiased outlet for it. As I mentioned, this situation required us to think of other points on the globe that had yet to be affected by the poor performance of *Puzzle Place.* It was not a lot different from my first dealings with *Thomas the Tank Engine.* I spoke with Emilia Nuccio, TibECo's executive director of international, and discussed the fate of this rather incredible children's' series. As of the writing of this book, Emilia has signed *Tots TV* into several countries in Latin America through both terrestrial and satellite television systems and has done several deals for merchandising. Additionally, we were now talking with potential broadcasters that specialize in Hispanic audiences for the U.S. market in order to tap into a new unbiased North American audience for this series.

Tots TV is now on track because Ragdoll and Emilia discussed the possibilities with each of these new broadcasters for reversioning the series so that the characters could assist in teaching other languages to kids: Portuguese/English, Portuguese/Spanish, Spanish/English. Because each show is being tailored to that individual market, the programmer and ultimately the child viewing has a sense of ownership, and we have a new way of presenting this great programming to broadcasters and the retail community. The additional thing to remember is that the problem was not with *Tots TV* but with the market conditions surrounding *Tots TV.* By finding a clean market or a new way to present the series to an existing market we were able to reintroduce the project to a new nonbiased audience.

Being true to your audience is simple once you determine who your audience is. Ask yourself these questions to build the last wall of your house and to help narrow your focus on your end user:

1. What do you offer?
2. Who does it appeal to?

3. Who is your competition?
4. Who does your competition appeal to?
5. What do you do better than your competition?
6. What is the one thing that differentiates your end user from your competition's end user?
7. What is the bit that makes you passionate about what you do? (Answering "money" won't work here. You have to dig deep to find out what it is about what you offer that you will not compromise, regardless of the cost.)
8. How does your answer to question 7 benefit your end user?

Your end user is: _____

The other questions to keep in mind are:

9. Who makes the purchase decision?
10. What is most important to the purchaser?

Remember that distraction and compromise can cost you your most valuable commodity...your end user.

Promotion, Promoción, Promotionae

It all comes down to appearances.

The biggest issue with most companies is that they do not spend enough monies to promote their brands. I, on the other extreme, have been accused of spending too much. A common business strategy is to put a percentage of anywhere from 3 to 5 percent of your annual budget into the advertising and promotion of your product or service. In my personal opinion, this business model only works if your company is the size of IBM. Whether yours is a small or large company or something in-between, success is predicated on your ability to expose your product or service to your audience. The perception of being able to compete with others is often more important than the reality. How can every retailer have the lowest price? Impossible—right? Read today's *New York Times* or your local Sunday paper and see how retailers are suggesting that *they,* in fact, have the lowest price not their competitor. If you are unwilling to believe that perception is reality then you might as well move to the next chapter (and let your competitors read on).

The itsy bitsy Entertainment Company believes very strongly in investing in the future of the brands it markets. Although I appreciate that this is a hot topic right now, we have been doing it for the past 5 years. IT'S THE ONLY WAY I KNOW HOW TO EXPOSE A BRAND TO THE MARKETPLACE. I believe that our possible customers (retailers) and their consumers want to see that the "owner" of the brand is supporting their own product. The "marketer" must be willing to put their money where their mouth is.

In order to secure a brand's long-term potential, each project that we represent has a marketing plan and a specific investment plan attached to it. We usually seed the market for a period, prior to introducing a property/product. With *Noddy,* for example, we teased the market for almost 4 years before we presented them with an opportunity to buy anything. Knowing that *Noddy* was perceived to be possibly "too British" for American audiences, we kept pushing the images of *Noddy* in the press and local trade publications. Our hope was that after continued exposure to the characters, the market would in time forget that *Noddy* was not American. That of course is an oversimplification to the marketing strategy of the brand, but I hope the concept is not lost.

Appearance Is Important

The itsy bitsy Entertainment Company needed to manifest that we were both forward thinkers and leaders in our specialization. As a result of our budgets being so small (so small that my mother used to say that we didn't have two nickels to rub together to keep warm), I had to create the perception of being bigger. I wasn't sure about what to do, so I went back to my childhood for the answers. Two particular experiences came to mind; a moment with my dad, and an episode in the television series, *Dynasty.*

When I was about 8 years old, I remember going with my dad to play tennis. He had on a really colorful and apparently expensive warm-up suit. I thought he must be a really great player (of course he was my dad!) and he told me that if you want to be a player you have to dress the part. He said that it doesn't matter if you know how to play the game as long as you look like you know how to play the game. Basically he was suggesting that I psych out my competition. Of course I was too young to understand at the time and that statement became a brainteaser for me for a number of years.

Several years later, I was watching an episode of *Dynasty*—the one where Blake loses it all. It appeared that they were going to have to leave the mansion (*I* was devastated so you can just imagine how disturbing it was for Blake and Crystal). Suddenly Blake walks into the room that Crystal has been sitting in looking tortured and he tells her to take out her best jewels and champagne flutes, because "we are going to have a big party." Crystal is flabbergasted and wonders if Blake has lost it. Damn it, doesn't he understand that they are on the verge of bankruptcy? Blake tells Crystal something to the effect that if you don't look rich people won't believe that you are rich. People want to back a winner. Needless to say they throw the party of the century, and it was a smash. They not only get to keep the house they become filthy rich (again). Every external communication we have undertaken at TibECo whether it is an ad campaign or an event at retail or even the launch of a new project/product, we consider the "dynasty strategy" before taking our first steps. "If you want your company to get the part, they have to project the part."

TibECo's first project (April 1995) was an extremely beautiful yet rather unknown book entitled *Miss Spider* by David Kirk. I took it as a sign from above that 2 days after I signed on to work with them, Madonna announced that she was going read *Miss Spider* on national TV (in her nightgown) to promote her latest CD, *Bedtime Stories*. If I had any doubt about the power of promotion and properly managed exposure, it rapidly evaporated after that. The one memory from that time that remains especially strong is the picture of Madonna reading her copy of *Miss Spider* on the front page of the Arts & Leisure section of *The New York Times*. It was immediately following that article that *Miss Spider* became an overnight sensation—at least in children's literary circles.

Our company's first big event was for *Miss Spider.* It was at Toy Fair 1996, which was held in New York City in February of that year. We had an arrangement with our partners at Scholastic (the publisher) and Callaway Publications (the book packager and rights holders) to put some monies behind the consumer marketing campaign. We were concerned that if we opened a showroom at Toy Fair and put up a display, we could possibly get lost in the crowd. The big challenge for our little company was how could we create something that would turn our book character into something that would compete with the giant properties from Disney, Warner, and Nickelodeon. We had *Miss Spider*'s great illustrations and wonderful story, and yet the truth was that *Miss Spider* was going to have to compete with very well established characters like Elmo and Mickey Mouse. Somehow this project was going to have to stand out from the sea of other properties vying for the attention of the key buyers, manufacturers and press that were attending the Toy Fair. We needed to find some unique way of promoting our character.

I had seen a promotion a few weeks prior to Toy Fair that inspired me. I was walking by the grand opening of a Duane Reade (drugstore chain in New York City) and saw that the opening was being covered as an editorial on the whole front page of *The New York Post*. New York tabloid newspapers are infamous for putting out outrageous cover stories such as "Headless Body Found in Topless Bar." But a drugstore opening? Something was out of whack. What Duane Reade had done was put a false cover over the real first page. Even I the skeptic of all skeptics was fooled (only for a couple of seconds, but fooled is fooled). I saw an opportunity there, and what a great promotional opportunity indeed! This was so clearly a case where perception was not reality.

Within hours, we had worked out a quantity and a price with *The New York Post* for them to create newspapers with a false cover that we could then hand out to buyers attending the first day of Toy Fair. This wasn't something that had been done before in our industry and something that 99+ percent of the populace don't know you can do. Even their promotion department wasn't quite sure, at first, how to handle the request. We provided them with all the materials. We made up a great tabloid headline— "Miss Spider to Marry Mr. Wright" (the theme of her new book *Miss Spider's Wedding*) and wrote the copy and created the graphics to go along with it. They printed up 2500 copies of our paper and sure enough, on the first day of Toy Fair, buyers attending the show were greeted by *New York Post* newspaper hawkers (actually a mixture of our staff and a variety of out-of-work actors). The scandalous Ms. Spider cover story on an actual edition of *The New York Post* cost us about $3000, and made more of an impact than the multitude of ads and billboards that the larger players had taken. Everyone walking the Toy Fair was talking about it. Somehow, on a shoestring budget, we had made her the center of attention.

To complement this, we threw an event at FAO Schwarz, the preeminent toy store in the country (if not the world). Collectively we hosted the actual wedding of Miss Spider and Holly Wright (the rather intellectual type of bug who won her heart). The event had about fifteen hundred guests including key buyers, press, and manufacturers. FAO closed the store for the evening and purchased exclusive products for the event. Buyers who had not received their invitations were standing out in the street insisting that they be let in. It was a sensation that was covered extensively in the media. I think the best person to describe this event and subsequent partnerships is David Niggli, chief operating officer of FAO Schwarz. He was there in the beginning (of time) and has worked with us through many of our in-store promotions, including events for...

Miss Spider's wedding...

The party was thrown to debut the Miss Spider's wedding book. It was right around Toy Fair time. Miss Spider had been very strong in the kid's publishing world. It was a very good book coming out of nowhere and it really took off. The event that The itsy bitsy Entertainment Company did at Toy Fair was to really create Miss Spider's wedding and Kenn went out and he hired a theatrical troupe that had wild costumes such as big spider heads and all the different bug characters from the book. They recreated the wedding in the store, as opposed to just an industry party where people were just coming in to meet and greet the authors and see the boutique. He created a theatrical experience for an event that got picked up in the press because it was an event, it wasn't a typical sort of the event, that says here it is, unveil, here's the book, go home kind of thing. They really created the theatrical event. I think the main thing is that Kenn is a master showman. He touches all aspects of the way of life in this country.

The Teletubbies...

When you look at Teletubbies *he was able to get to pretty much every facet of the population whether it was parents, little kids, teenagers. Everybody knew about* Teletubbies *when it came here. That whole advance buzz that Kenn got, not only the trade toy books that basically go to industry people. But Kenn got* Teletubbies *picked up in lifestyle sections and in fashion magazines and every newspaper and every television show was talking about* Teletubbies. *He had this way of creating a buzz that's very theatrical, it's sort of like the entertainment business as opposed to the typical product launch, and I think that was the success of* Teletubbies. *I think the program is very good, don't take me wrong. But to realize that a phenomenon takes a lot more people than just the 2-year-olds of the world. We launched the product in May and there was a line waiting and the program* [television show on PBS] *had just gone on in April. When you look at the past history of the toy world it's a fourth-quarter business. You couldn't really launch products outside of that and here was a product being launched in May, which is not a toy season and you're selling thousands and thousands of pieces across the country in every location.*

Just a few years ago you wouldn't see people doing that much in the toy world. No one wants to be part of it unless it's the holiday. I mean even the fact that when we did the first Teletubbies [Hasbro's Talking Teletubbies toys] *in the plexiglass cases and created a brand-new toy with Kenn's signature on it that we were able to sell for $50—and at that point no one even knew Kenn. We all knew who he was in the industry but I don't think the average customer did. They delivered the first toys in armored trucks and I remember some people from other retailers freaking out because they didn't have it. It was crazy, people just grabbed them like they were going out of style because he had created this marketing phenomenon around Ragdoll's television series that everybody* *wanted to get a piece of. With that kind of demand and that kind of onslaught of publicity, people want it then, they want it now, your child wants it now, they can't wait. And they're buying all of them at once. It wasn't like they were buying one, they had to have multiples, they had to have all of them.*

And the in-store experience was different. It was the first time we had really done side windows in sort of a 3-D relief. We were able to create a three-dimensional Teletubbies or a feeling of a three dimension and we had the TV in their stomachs and you had that complete feeling going down the street. I think Kenn knows exactly what he wants with the properties he markets. He's thought it out. He has a definite vision of what it needs to be. It was an environment, it wasn't just about, and here's a sign that said Teletubbies. I mean, we had the hill with voice trumpets. We had rabbits. And then you got to the top of the escalator and you had four foam sculptures of the Teletubbies and there was the hill and the house and everything. It was really about creating an environment that reflected the program so when a child or an adult went into it they felt like they were really going into Teletubbyland. And even on the side windows it was the same thing that reflected all the aspects of the show. But it was very much directed—vision is what it is—that's what makes great properties—there is somebody there that gives it a good sense of direction. And quite often you'll find with an entertainment company, the marketing group has one vision, the licensing group had another vision, the head has a vision, and the artistic people have another. I generally have found that everybody at TibECo seems to be on board with the same vision and I think Kenn is very clear in what he sees where this thing wants to go. Which is helpful for people like me and the people that work for him so you don't have to go through and try to figure out what people want.

You don't have a dominant individual like he is, whether it's in the entertainment or the licensing world. He reminds me of Louis B. Mayer. He was a big theatrical producer. He pulled all the stops out, whether the show was a hit or not, everybody knew about his show because of what he did. And I think Kenn is like that, you can feel his passion about what he does, and he goes to the "nth" degree but he's definitely so strong in his conviction of what he wants to do. I think it's been great for the toy industry because of that— because I don't think the toy industry has a lot of people like that and they need more people like that—people that want to think out of the box and create excitement—especially if you're in the kids' business. These kids are inundated. When we were growing up you had three stations and that was about it. Now you've got 100 different cable stations, you've got the Internet, you've got all the different aspects of music, television, movies that they're exposed to. You need to get your message across because they're looking at those things and you can't just sneak in. There's a few that get in there but it's never at that magnitude.

The simple things you might have been able to get away with, particularly in the licensing world in the past, I don't think thrive anymore. The days of logo slapping are long gone. It has to be innovative product and also if you're tying it in with a brand or a character base, it's got to reflect what you see in that program so you just can't slap it together. You've got to say OK that's an item that I can recreate from the show or whatever.

I know Kenn searches the world over for properties. I think he's probably one of the most knowledgeable people in terms of all the different forms of entertainment for kids. I trust him. If he's going after something, I certainly want to explore it and see what he's up to, because his track record is there. I think he does his homework before he gets involved in a property and has a good sense of it before he just signs on the line. If you think about it, he has done everything.

And the *Eloise* launch party at The Plaza, of course!

That evening I kept calling everybody in my office and saying come look what he's up to now. Look what he's done—The Plaza is pink! It was spectacular. I think everybody was just knocked out. It was great theater again. He really kind of sweeps you away and you don't see people doing things like that anymore. It was done in the style of Eloise and I think when that property was being shopped around, he would've been my first choice to get it, because I think he could understand Eloise. There's a lot of people, particularly in Hollywood, that I was concerned might not understand Eloise because it is a sophisticated property and isn't just for a bratty little girl. There's a lot of adult humor in it that can be adapted for kids that you don't want to lose the aspects because then she's not Eloise anymore. And I think that with the kind of event he staged captured it and people walked away knocked out and talking a lot about Eloise. People are buzzing about Eloise and obviously it has a larger than life quality and then you get people that just happen to be walking by The Plaza and go, "What is that? Why is the Plaza pink?" "Why is there a truck outside FAO Schwartz?" All of the sudden you find that people are buying this stuff that you never thought in their lives would be buying a Teletubby or looking to buy an Eloise doll. It creates a theater where people are walking by and go, "Wow! What is it?" That's the best thing you can have because then they want to be a part of it. They want to feel what's new at the top. I think that's just going to even get more and more so because of the Internet and that shopping is so convenient now out of your home. I do not believe the consumer is going to stop shopping, they're just going to make sure that where they shop is going to be special and unique and different. It's got to be an experience that I can't get sitting in front of my computer. I think that is why people like working with Kenn, who can deliver and will continue to deliver going forward.

Get The Word Out

I remember reading a really fantastic little fact: During WWI starving women, if forced to choose between a loaf of bread and a tube of lipstick, were more likely to purchase a lipstick. Based on that analogy a public relations firm is my tube of lipstick. I do not think a small company can survive without an effective PR firm out there trying to increase your profile and help build awareness for your company. After Dean (my suit) and Dana (my assistant/secretary), the next "person" I hired was my public relations company.

Many companies believe that the last place to add to or the first place to cut during a start-up or slowdown is the advertising and promotion and public relations area. I could not disagree more strongly. The time you need to promote your company the most is when you are starting out or when business is bad. Once you are a huge success and everyone knows who you are, you can sit back a bit—but not too much because there is always someone out there trying to throw you off the precipice.

I approach publicity the same way that I approach everything else. Who is the end user and what is their mission? The media has two masters: the writer and the reader. I've found that the writer likes someone who is not afraid to speak their mind and whose candor will support their focus. They also like to know that the person is fair-minded and will stick to his or her beliefs. I have basically created a persona for the media—someone who is outspoken and knowledgeable, yet friendly and approachable. I have above all else become an "expert" in a limited field.

My first agency, HWH Public Relations, had a unique mission. They had to create something for my new company. A company that had no product. They could sell a concept or sell me as a leader, or they could sell a company that was breaking new ground. Lois Whitman (the head of the organization) recognized these items as opportunities and worked with me to create the type of industry profiles I needed to launch my new venture. Lois and company went out of their way to get TibECo some type of profile. I never met a bigger hustler in my life than Lois Whitman. Unfortunately, we hit the proverbial financial rough patch. We simply didn't have any money left and were forced to tell Lois that we couldn't afford to pay them their retainer for a couple of months. However, I had a deal (an offer that they couldn't refuse or so I thought). If they would float us for 2 months, we would double their monthly retainer. We knew that we had monies coming due within 60 days. After a great deal of thought, Lois told us that they were not able to agree to my new payment plan. I realized I was behaving a lot like Wimpy—"Please sir can I have a hamburger today for which I will gladly pay you tomorrow?" Despite tremendous mutual respect and a solid working relationship, we had to part company. So now I had to find another option. As a little side note, years later, Lois called and asked me to speak at an event she was throwing at the New York Friar's Club. She pulled me aside to tell me that she had always regretted not taking the risk, but that she is proud to have been with me at the very beginning.

After I left Lois's company, the monies did come in and I went shopping for a new publicist. I had heard about Rubenstein Public Relations. They were the folks who represented some of the biggest moguls in the world. They had a high-powered office on Sixth Avenue. It was so farfetched to think that I could afford to hire them or that they would be interested in me as a client. Nonetheless, we called and made an appointment to meet with Richard Rubenstein (nothing ventured nothing gained). Rather surprisingly, Richard immediately got what I was trying to achieve and agreed to take us on as a client. I loved walking around town telling people that Rubenstein represented The Donald, Rupert Murdoch, and...me.

This was just prior to Licensing Show 1996 and one of the first pieces of ink they were able to get was a full-page story in the purple section of *USA Today*. The article was about *Tots TV* joining the PBS lineup for fall. The timing was perfect! And as we know in business, timing is everything. It was the first day of the PBS Annual Meeting, a meeting that attracted every top PBS executive from around the country, and as luck would have it the first day of Licensing Show in New York.

So the investment in public relations paid off for us in just that one story. Every key broadcast partner immediately knew us, and the investment community came to check out who we were at the Licensing Show. Richard also helped us focus on our business press, agreeing with me that if we were going to succeed we needed to be seen by the people in the investment community. With their help we were written up in several of the biggest business publications in the business (and several of the small ones).

Sometimes an opportunity for a story in the press or some other outlet for exposure may present itself that seems too good to pass up. The only problem is that the timing is not right. If the timing is not right then the story is not right: Full period, end, and stop! Timing is everything. In fact there is a stupid little PR joke that says there are three rules to PR: (1) timing, (2) timing, and of course (3) timing.

With the launch of *Teletubbies* in America, we were faced with just such a dilemma. In the early summer of 1997, while I was still in negotiations with PBS about airing the series, I received a surprise call from a reporter from *The Wall Street Journal* wanting to run a piece about *Teletubbies*. *Teletubbies* had premiered on the BBC in the United Kingdom in March of 1997 and from the first day it was a huge magnet to controversy; however, it was an unknown in America. The reporter, Robert Frank, was based in London and had seen the phenomenon that was happening there. He made some inquiries in the United Kingdom about the series with Ragdoll (the series creators) and they had sent him to me, as we were the ones charged with handling the media throughout the Americas. It was clear that this story could have huge ramifications if not handled properly. Unfortunately, although I would have loved (given my right arm is more like it) to do a major story with *The Wall Street Journal*, I knew that the timing was not right and didn't feel that it was right to cooperate on a story at that time.

Mr. Frank, to his credit, was relentless. He had started calling in early May, and Eileen Potrock, TibECo's executive director of marketing was able to hold him off for several weeks. He was persistent and thought about writing the story without our cooperation. We knew that if the story went out too early or if the press attacked the series for being geared to children as young as 1, prior to seeing how children respond to it, the press would have turned on *Teletubbies* and start to attack the credibility of this extraordinary series. Even if it meant alienating *The Wall Street Journal*, we could not support this story and had to do whatever necessary to stop it from running. I was close to closing the deal with PBS and I did not want to do something that would interrupt that progress; additionally there had been a great deal of interest in Teletubbies coming out of the Licensing Show (especially from Mike Goldstein the CEO of Toys "R" Us).

I knew that it would be a good time to get the press if we could manage the story and make sure that it fairly represented the quality and originality of the series. We were not worried about whether children and their families would like *Teletubbies* (we knew they would); our only concern was that the media portray the series accurately. We were not looking for a free ride; we simply knew that a biased story could impact the series' success. A negative impact was of particular concern, because the series was not airing on television and therefore the viewer wasn't able to turn on the series and form their own opinion. Robert and Eileen struck a deal. He delayed running his piece until later in the summer, and we provided him with access to the creators. We asked for a couple of other things regarding placement and he asked us to provide some of the forward strategy for the Teletubbies brand off the screen. Robert met with Anne Wood and Andrew Davenport, and observed them at work. I spent a couple of hours on the phone with him, talking about what our goals were for the program and the offscreen product in the Americas. Robert, in return, delivered the front-page center for the story. This one article, which appeared on August 21, 1997, was a turning point for our company. And the timing was everything.

There are several great press stories that have come since, however none of them were as monumental as *The Wall Street Journal* piece because of the instant awareness and potential it offered. I did have one other favorite moment though. One morning, Eileen got calls from *Good Morning America*, *The Today Show*, and CNN, all wanting to do stories. Because of the tight schedule of all the principals involved in the series and the actual production schedule, Eileen *had the ability to select only two* for on-site shoots. (We later satisfied the last outlet with separate interviews with the creators—we certainly didn't want to miss out on this possible opportunity.)

In working with the media, I have always made it a rule to be fair, open, and not afraid to confront the issues. I have continued to stay true to that philosophy no matter the personal stake. We've had dozens of scandals over the past several months, and through them all I have tried to take the high road while never forsaking my responsibilities to the properties I represent. The two most frightening issues that I had to deal with were the Talking Po fiasco and the nonsense with Jerry Falwell.

The Talking Po fiasco was very disturbing for me, because it showed me how sensationalized our media has become. This all started with a phone call from a mother of a young child who insisted we give her four free toys, or she was going to tell the media that her child's Talking Po doll said obscenities. It felt like blackmail and we held our ground. This mother, true to her word, called the press to say that the Po doll was polluting her child's mind. Ragdoll Limited, Hasbro, and PBS all stand for providing the very best in nonviolent, educational, fun, and funny programming for the youngest of children. Because of this incident, I wound up in the back seat of a taxi in London having to bestow the virtues of this rather glorious and extremely harmless children's series to members of the American press. All this because one member of the press could not resist the headlines they would receive from this unsubstantiated story.

And just when I thought that the media's Teletubby witch hunt was starting to calm down, Reverend Jerry Falwell came out with the story that Tinky Winky was gay. How positively absurd, and yet the media had a field day. It actually once again became the second most written story in America in 1999, second only to President Clinton's impeachment trial. Having to go on *The Today Show* was the single hardest moment of my professional career. I couldn't believe how political the world had become. And for the first time I understood how Michael Jackson could actually have been innocent. To be wrongfully accused of something is absolutely insane and here it was all going to play out on the screen—worldwide. In my heart I believe that Falwell was trying to use the publicity and notoriety of the Teletubbies to get national exposure for both his website and for his ministry in general. All of my advisers told me not to go on television and to absolutely avoid the story (which inadvertently was breaking right in the middle of Toy Fair). Yet somehow I felt that I would be betraying my responsibilities to my clients and the children we vowed to serve, so despite my advisers' advice, I went on and defended their (the Teletubbies') honor. Instead of going on the defense, we put a full court press on this issue. I refused to allow caregivers to be mislead or taken advantage of. I wanted to make sure that American families understood this media frenzy for the political issue that it was and how it had really nothing to do with the Teletubbies at all. This was not the first time that either Anne or I had to deal with people riding on the back of her success, and we were determined to defend her work to the bitter end if necessary. And to my total amazement, Reverend Falwell backed down and actually apologized on *The Today Show*. I'm not sure that I understand what actually happened, but I know that something happened. It all felt like a dream and yet, to this day, I still look over my shoulder, waiting for the other shoe to drop.

As a result of all the media attention, we now have an internal Public Relations Department, overseeing our agencies and working with our various partners to coordinate story ideas and to get coverage for the events for which we have become famous.

One of my most familiar quotes around the office is, "The party starts with the invitation." I really believe that you create the tone and the expectations for an event or a trade show exhibit the moment people first hear about it. Our company is now known for being great promoters, and we do make it seem easy. Only we know the detail work it takes to make something seem so simple. After years of doing these star-studded events and promotions, I truly understand that simplicity is the highest art form.

Recreating Your Image for the First Time

At trade shows, most companies build a booth, and take it from show to show, year after year, putting the same message out over and over again. Our company takes a different tack. We want to create a stir; after all, we are part of the entertainment business, and entertain is a key part of that phrase. So each year we totally remake our booth with a different theme and different environment, never losing sight of our audience.

Our company's first Licensing Show was in 1996. We had limited funds and I went to our CFO and we talked about monies. We had $130,000 in the bank; I needed at least $120,000 for our first exhibit at the Licensing Show. After he got up off the floor, Dean agreed with me that if we were going down then let's go down in a blaze of glory (remember my story about Blake and Crystal). We needed to get the exposure. I was worried that our finances were dwindling away and that we needed to do something drastic to get attention before we had nothing left.

So I went about developing our first exhibit. We wanted people to understand our corporate philosophy so we created a booth were everything was oversized—like *Land of the Giants* I wanted adults to feel very small. Everything was made of kid's stuff. The table was a giant lollipop and the seats were huge whistles. We even had an 8-foot-tall gumball machine. On each of the 12 huge building blocks we stenciled in our properties' names and added some graphics and television monitors. The night before the show, we found out that PBS had committed to airing *Tots TV,* so we spent several hours stenciling the words "Premiering on PBS Fall 1996" on all of our blocks.

The second year allowed us to create "Itsybitsyville," population 20 (give or take). We had grown in size and in stature. In this park-like setting, we were able to put up billboards of our properties soaring as high as 18 feet, complete with moving parts, neon lights, and a bubble machine that tended to get a bit overactive at times. We also set up picnic tables for meetings and rented thousands of dollars of trees for the 3-day show. We had a very successful show (except for that darn bubble machine).

Our third year gave us an opportunity to expand beyond the booth. Licensing 1998 had the first-ever bus routes named after each of our children's properties. There was the Teletubbies route, the Noddy route, the Tots TV route and The itsy bitsy Entertainment route (for our smaller properties to be highlighted). Everyone attending the shows from all the key hotels had to find her or his special TibECo bus route; also, these buses went around midtown Manhattan for a week, allowing additional public exposure. There were a variety of other sponsorships as well.

The highlight was clearly the canvas bags with the special three-dimensional Teletubbies image. Because we acquired the rights to the exclusive show bags, we were also able to control their contents. Only our materials went inside the bag (with the exception of a trade publication that put their magazine in the bag in exchange for free ads in their daily newsmagazine). This bag was handed out to every attendee. There was such a craze that the show's promoters had to create a special system to make sure that people got only one bag.

Our booth that year was a bit more low key. It was The itsy bitsy Museum, with the original characters from each of the shows we represent. Of course our booth came with some futuristic furniture and suspended from the ceilings were three flat-screen 40-inch television screens with touch pad videodisc recordings of each of our represented properties.

By our fourth year we took the largest booth space in the convention creating our own circus. Complete with a 60- by 60-foot blue and white striped tent, light shows, and cages (including one lion's cage for my meetings with a special sign stating "please do not feed the CEO"); landscaping with Teletubbies topiaries, a Noddy Carousel, and a center ring. Our circus was turned into the focal point of the show, with even our competition identifying themselves by their relationship to our booth in the hall ("Look for me two aisles to the right of the itsy bitsy Entertainment tent"). True to form, we made sure that everyone who might arrive at the show knew who was throwing the party. We once again sponsored the buses, wrapped the stairs (and this time the banisters and table tops too!); provided a special Teletubbies neck wallet; and created a three-dimensional Noddy briefcase, complete with a bell. To top it off, we started the licensing show by having Noddy ring the bell opening the New York Stock Exchange (a very long story).

As I said previously, I believe that the party begins when the invitees receive their invitations. At The itsy bitsy Entertainment

Company, we take our parties very seriously, as serious as a heart attack. In the past 5 years, we've had four large launch parties and many smaller ones. The large parties have always taken place in a landmark location and we've tried to up the ante every time.

Our *Tots TV* launch was held at The New York Public Library. The invitations were designed as self-mailers and opened to show our corporate blue and white stripes along with the Tots and their logo inviting everyone in a colorful way to celebrate their premiere on PBS. When everyone arrived they came into a room with refreshments—Tots TV–colored popcorn (green, red, and blue), a video wall, and a short presentation from both Alice Cahn, director of children's programming from PBS, and me. We then introduced them to a short screening of the *Tots TV* series. When the presentation was over, the doors opened and dozens of entertainers brought our guests (businesspeople and their children) into the main room of the library were we held a carnival with crafts and activities. Our party was about a children's show, but it was also about children, and we made sure that children attended this event so that the adults could understand the magical qualities of the series. We also made sure that the children would get the same type of enjoyment from the party as they did from the show.

Our next ambitious party was for *Teletubbies*. For the *Teletubbies* launch we created special oversized invitations that included a mask of an individual Teletubby. These masks were then sent out to over 5000 people around the country, inviting them to attend the launch party with their children. For the party, we took over Roseland Dance Hall, famous in New York for being the best dance hall in the city during the forties and fifties. The Teletubbies love to dance and the venue was enormous so this choice was perfect.

To plan this party, we paid attention to every minutia of detail. What was the experience that people would get as they walked down the street toward the entrance? How would anyone standing on line be entertained? How would they be led to the coat check and then to the main floor? What aspects of the series would we bring to life, because the Teletubbies themselves never leave Teletubbyland?

What would they be able to take away as a remembrance of the evening? And most of all, we needed to understand what the space was and how we could make it a special experience for the children.

We decorated Roseland to make it into our own version of Teletubbyland, using the colors from the series, but not trying to actually recreate the series. We made sure that there was entertainment throughout the party. Teletubbies is about living in a technological world and we worked with a company to set up touch screen displays where children (and adults) could explore the world of Teletubbyland. We hired a 25-piece band and brought in a petting zoo. We had a Caribbean steel band playing in the area of the coat check and bathrooms. For my staff, I created special Teletubbies shirts, which were black dress shirts with a special embroidered design of the four Teletubbies on the back. For our licensing and broadcast partners, we created the same embroidery on a white dress shirt.

During the presentation, I was able to introduce the Teletubbies to America, but it was through the technological magic of two large video walls, rather than through live appearances. And for the children, we mounted television sets closer to their height, so they could sit down and watch what was sure to become their favorite characters. We also created a photo area, where children (and adults) could have their pictures put into the tummy of their favorite Teletubby. A whopping 3000 adults and children attended this party, along with news crews from the three New York network affiliates, E!, CNN, and Access Hollywood, and reporters from *The New York Times, People* magazine, and *USA Today* to name a few.

As part of the experience we wanted to make sure that everyone who left our Teletubbies launch party had a special gift. What should have been the easiest part of this party, turned into the most frustrating. This was an area where we had to be the most creative. Because we had no Teletubbies product in America yet, we decided to import product created for the United Kingdom for the event. We ordered the backpacks, which were being made in Hong Kong, with plenty of time for delivery. In fact, they were shipped out early and made it to America with time to spare, but the factory had put the wrong classification on the visa and customs was holding our Teletubbies gifts hostage! My staff went above and beyond, staying up until the middle of the night to call Hong Kong each day, and then to call the folks in China (Hong Kong had just come under Chinese rule) to get a new visa processed. We were on phones to embassies and went as far as to state that it would be a terrible thing if word got out that the U.S. and Chinese governments had no heart about gifts that were going to little children. (We had planned to donate any leftover gifts to a children's charity.) In fact, a member of my staff even went out to the customs warehouse at JFK Airport to beg them to release the shipment and we asked our partners at Hasbro if they could help.

Sure enough, on the day of the party we got a call from our customs broker that the bags would be released at 2 P.M. We had trucks ready and when the first shipment of boxes arrived at Roseland at 4 P.M., a cheer went up from our entire staff. It was worth every bit of it, because one of the guests who received and wore her Teletubbies backpack home was Lawrie Miflin, the television writer for *The New York Times*. As Lawrie told me later, that backpack made her a believer in Teletubbies. She wore it on the New York subway, and was approached on the platform by a couple of teenagers (which, in New York, can be a bit disconcerting). They not only knew about the Teletubbies, but also knew the character she was carrying. Of course, Lawrie thought it might be a fluke that these particular teens knew about the show and that perhaps I had put them up to it (you see Lawrie knows me really well). When she got on the train, she was approached by a different group of children who also knew about the Teletubbies. It helped Lawrie realize what a phenomenon the show really was, and if it wasn't for the work of my staff in getting those backpacks to the party, the article Lawrie wrote about our series may never have happened.

Our most recent party was in conjunction with our company acquiring the rights to Eloise. Eloise had been out of circulation for 20 years and this past June, there was one of Hollywood's most fiercely competitive bidding wars of the past decade for the property. After some 16 weeks of negotiation and some very tough competition (apparently Disney, Warner Brothers, and several well-known production companies like those of Tom Hanks and Meg Ryan were vying for the rights), TibECo won the rights to the movies, broadcast, and merchandising of the world's most famous 6-year-old girl. In celebration of this and the reintroduction of the Eloise books and the limited introduction of Eloise product at FAO Schwarz for Christmas 1999, I felt the time was right to welcome Eloise back to the Plaza. Invitations went out for the event, printed on Tiffany's paper stock, with Eloise's familiar handwriting over the engraving demanding that people come to her party. For the first time in their history, the Plaza closed down the whole public area of the Fifth Avenue side of their hotel, and we created the Eloise Pink & Black Debutante Ball. A 20-foot high replica of Eloise in front of the pink bathed Plaza hotel, complete with pink carpet, greeted guests who arrived. As they were led inside, they were given special Eloise credentials, on either pink or black satin ribbons, which gave them access to the party. We had draped off the Plaza's famous Palm Court with pink satin and provided the waiters with pink gloves. Over 10,000 pink roses were flown in from South America, transforming the Palm Court and the connecting Terrace Room into an oasis of pink. We produced a special 45-minute documentary with people, both famous and not, talking about Eloise and what she had meant to them, that played on monitors around the rooms. Additionally we had a 10-piece string orchestra playing in the room downstairs and the most exotic and glorious foods flown in from around the world placed at stations around the room, as well as passed by waiters through the crowd. In the middle of it all, we hired Joan Rivers as our roving reporter, interviewing guests.

My presentation was scripted, which was a first for me. I am used to speaking in public and hate to read from a script, but it was my idea to make this presentation interactive with both pretaped and live segments, so I had to provide the director with cues. I introduced the various dignitaries from Simon & Schuster, Hilary Knight, who drew Eloise on her adventures, Don Gold president of TibECo's theatrical division and the extraordinary film producer Denise Di Novi who is producing the first two Eloise films for us.

Denise and Don then introduced the writing team whose last project, the *Rugrats* movie, grossed more than $100,000,000 domestically. After the presentation I invited everyone (all 1500 guests) to join us upstairs in the Grand Ballroom for flaming baked Alaska and dancing to our society orchestra (after all, it was Eloise's ball).

All of this may seem a bit over the top, but remember that TibECo is an entertainment company and it is important for others to perceive us as experts in the art of entertaining. Regardless, it is not the size of the event—it is the commitment to detail that will make any event, exhibit, or party you throw a success. It's that attention and the ability to make your guest or client feel a sense of privilege to work with you that will put you a few steps ahead of the others.

I find that the only way to make people understand your industry is to make them a part of your industry. In my case it is slightly easier, because everyone wants to be in show business. In every promotion we do we try to give a little piece of Hollywood to our guests.

Take the time to complete the following few questions prior to putting together your next exhibit or event.

1. What message are you trying to send?
2. To whom are you sending it?
3. How do you want that person to walk away from your message feeling?
4. After answering the previous questions, think about what you can do to make your message have that certain uniqueness, which will create a lasting impression.

Remember that promotion is your roof—and the sky's the limit!

7

Understand Your Universe

Make sure to line your ducks in a row,
but be careful not to become a sitting duck.

I must have said three thousand times throughout this book how difficult it is for a small company (or a new-product introduction) to survive in today's cruel, cruel business world. In fact, I've said it so many times that I am getting bored of writing it, so I can only imagine how boring it must be to read. Nonetheless, I will keep saying it because I believe that people should not naively enter into the decision to mortgage their lives and put everything on the line without seriously contemplating the risks. Regardless of your role in the business world, it is truly essential to understand the universe into which you are entering. Is there a lot of competition? Do you have the resources necessary? Do you know what you do not know? Do you know your audience? And equally important, is your idea/service unique? Do you know how you can make your start-up business or your new product feel important?

I think the biggest little secret that I can offer is "try to shape the universe differently." It can be very intimidating to try to take a new product to market, or to open a new business. The key is that you must not think of yourself as a small part of the big bad world. Instead, you must find a way to make yourself the big fish in the little sea. I know you just read that and said, "What did he just say?" So, let me try this again.

If you try to compete with the entire universe right now, you'll quickly find that you don't have the resources (either financial or human). However if you find a limited segment of the universe (in my case, it is preschool entertainment), you stand a chance of competing. It is not relevant whether the entire universe knows you (other than for your ego) if only a portion of that group is going to use your services anyway. What is important, however, is that you correctly reach out to the limited part of the universe that needs to have knowledge of your existence. Thomas the Tank Engine (TTE&F) changed the face of children's entertainment in America, and yet most Americans have never heard of him.

When we were marketing *Thomas the Tank Engine,* we knew that our resources were tight and that we could not compete with all of the massive entertainment companies that were out there (same old story). In order to make TTE&F a big fish in a small pond, we had to create a smaller universe for him. Instead of making him compete with *all* entertainment properties, we limited his world to PBS children's entertainment. We niched him into that smaller world only targeting customers that watched PBS or had small children. There was a great deal of goodwill between PBS and caregivers and they had a 20-year successful relationship as a result of their hit show, *Sesame Street,* and we knew that we needed to capitalize on that relationship. At the time, PBS's only hit show was *Sesame Street* and its offscreen sales were no longer setting any records. It was a perfect opportunity for TTE&F to enter the market as the big new kid on the small block. Thomas became a massive hit off the television screen and yet if you don't have a young boy (and to a lesser extent a young girl) between the ages of 3 to 6, you probably don't know him. We aimed all of our attention in our advertising and promotion to the caregivers of children under 7.

With all of *Thomas the Tank Engine*'s successes, the most rewarding for me was that somehow TTE&F gave parents "permission" to talk about their kids' entertainment with other parents. Not only was it a goal for us to bring preschool entertainment into the limelight, these grassroots conversations were the backbone of Thomas's commercial success.

Prior to Thomas, most caregivers expressed concern and, to a lesser degree, an interest in their children's entertainment. However the idea of talking about what their kids play with to other parents was, well frankly, not very likely. Then two things happened—a shortage of TTE&F die cast vehicles and an extraordinary event at Bloomingdales.

After researching PBS's demographics, we chose to limit the distribution of TTE&F products exclusively to the specialty channel. As a result of such a narrow channel it became increasingly difficult for consumers to find the products. Parents had to ask other parents "if you see that _____ TTE&F toy could you get an extra one for me?" Parents were talking and saying, "I didn't know your son liked that show…my son adores it…blah blah blah." Of course that happens all the time now, whether it is for Furby or Pokeman or the Teletubbies. However, 10 years ago, it was unusual. We knew that the most important thing for Thomas's long-term success was to build a grassroots campaign to get parents to talk about how much they approved of TTE&F and how much their kids liked it. I knew that all we had to do was get families together and our products/characters would speak for themselves. The bottom line is that if it was true that kids liked our characters and that parents were looking for healthy alternatives for their children, then all we needed to do was expose them to each other. If it wasn't true, well then all of the money on earth wouldn't/couldn't make a child like anything, so what did we have to lose?

The first time I threw an event with Bloomingdales for Thomas the Tank Engine, I knew that all of our efforts were going to pay off.

It was clearly the line of demarcation for his success. We were introducing new TTE&F toys, clothing, and accessories and Thomas was going to make his first-ever live appearance (well actually, it was a life-sized model of Thomas that had moving eyes and steam). We decided to hold it at Bloomingdales on 59th Street in New York City. We talked WNET (PBS's New York affiliate) into plugging the appearance for 1 week prior to the event. Our goal was simply to draw attention to this adorable children's series by getting word of mouth from different caregivers. Our hope was to have a couple of hundred parents and their children come to the store.

The morning of the event I arrived 2 hours early, only to see a sea of people outside—parents and their children, all waiting to meet their beloved character from their favorite show. People had been on line for 5 hours, having driven from as far away as Philadelphia. There were more than eighteen thousand people there, with lines wrapped around all four sides of the store (more than four city blocks). So many people that Bloomingdales had to close the elevators and escalators in the store. This was only the second time in the company's history (the only other time ironically was when the Queen of England had come to visit the store—and that was for security reasons). As you can imagine, because of the onslaught of parents and children, all of the merchandise (and I do mean *all* of the merchandise) sold within hours. And that should have been a good thing, but...

Unfortunately, a writer for *The New York Times* was there with her small child, and by the time she got into the store there wasn't anything left for her child. She got so angry that she dedicated her entire feature to attacking us for not having enough products, as if it were deliberate. Who could have possibly guessed that so many people would show up or that they would sell such incredible quantities of goods? This was a very scary time in my life. Our team had done everything right and yet an unforeseen event could have stopped Thomas dead in his tracks. We immediately put a spin on it with our publicist and my in-house marketing staff went out to set the record straight. We took the opportunity to show the industry how popular Thomas was at the grassroots level. Although our calls were never returned by *The New York Times* writer, we did start receiving hundreds of calls from various manufacturers and retailers inquiring about Thomas the Tank Engine products. And from that spark TTE&F was born.

One of the most influential people in the toy industry is Michael Goldstein, chief executive officer and chairman of the board of Toys "R" Us. I remember my first meeting with Michael as if it were yesterday. I was so nervous—he was a legend and I was not even worthy of the title "bit player." All I was, was a man on a mission. Michael remembers our first meeting quite differently. He kindly offered to share his experiences with Thomas the Tank Engine & Friends.

Our folks had been trying to meet with Kenn with no success on Thomas. I was the vice chairman of the company [Toys "R" Us] *at the time and I said, let me meet with him. Bob Weinberg advised me to make sure that I always refer to Thomas as Thomas or Thomas the Tank Engine. Never Thomas the Tank, because Kenn feels very strongly against war toys or anything that denotes a violent type of toy. And calling it Thomas the Tank made it sound like it was a GI Joe item, more than it really was. So the meeting went on and it's easy to say Thomas the Tank. So I guess after about an hour, hour and a half we were talking I said, in the conversation, Thomas the Tank and then I went Engine! And I saw that Kenn didn't laugh but he saw what happened. He saw that evidently I knew that I wasn't supposed to say it and then just as we were leaving it happened again and I went Thomas the Tank . . . Engine! I remember leaving his office and speaking to my wife that evening "I said you won't believe it, I'm the number two guy at Toys "R" Us,*

> *helping run this $8 billion dollar company and here's what*
> *happens, I'm just jumping around to make sure I never say*
> *"Thomas the Tank". And I knew that Kenn realized what*
> *was going on too and we laugh about it from time to time.*

It was incredible to me that Mike (Mr. Goldstein at that time) was willing to stop in to see me; however, it was extraordinary that he understood my goals for Thomas the Tank Engine and was keen to support them. As Mike said, I was aware that he had been coached not to say Thomas the Tank. I was really impressed that he took the time to meet me, but much more impressed that he was trying to show a sense of respect to what was important to me. I knew from his handshake that we had formed an alliance that would benefit both of us.

I truly underestimated the importance of the niche market that TTE&F had successfully mastered. When Mike called to meet with me, at first I was nervous and when that wore off, I recognized that we must have done something right. And that meant something special was going on here that I needed to exploit further. Because TRU was at the time the only freestanding toy chain in America, we didn't have to worry about class of trade restrictions or other legalities. *However,* I was concerned about the way the goods would be presented in their stores and some other marketing issues (I had come this far and built a solid and rather substantial business for Britt's company—I wasn't going to throw it all away nor in a rash or hasty decision). After a couple of other discussions, we expanded our niche market to include Toys "R" Us. This new alliance had a lot of potential.

I asked Michael to explain the retail terrain at the time we started working together.

> *In 1993 Toys "R" Us was leading the market in terms of the*
> *toy business. I think the Lionels and Child Worlds were*
> *either out of business or just about out of business. And*
> *then there was KB and some specialty shops. But the*

leading push was starting with the discount stores. The Wal-Marts and Targets and Kmarts were starting to increase their toy selections filling a void in the marketplace because everyone other than Toys "R" Us was pretty much out of business.

Toys "R" Us actually goes back 50 years. but the real growth of Toys "R" Us is about 20 years ago with rapid growth all through the 1980s and into the 1990s opening 30 to 40 stores a year and eventually getting to what we have now which is about 700 stores. So back in the period of 1992, 1993, we probably had 500 stores by then. And what was starting to occur and I think Kenn saw it happening, is that the discounters were using the toy items as just ways to get customers in the store. What they would do is take a strong selling toy and discount it. Give it away for a very low price and just try and hammer it out as a loss leader to bring customers into the store. The problem with that is twofold. One, it did nothing to develop the brand, in fact it actually hurt the brand because it looked like it was becoming a clearance item or giveaway and really didn't have intrinsic value. The second thing was that the whole ambiance of the brand became almost like a box of cereal in terms of here. It doesn't matter what it does, what it is, if people want it, just get a low price and sell it rather than romancing it and creating something special with it.

Kenn, in running Thomas at that time, was very concerned because he knew Thomas was a special toy line, a special license that moms and dads as well as kids loved. And he didn't believe that it was one that you needed to do extensive price promotions or giveaways for. He thought it was something that succeeded based on the most

*important thing in terms of a toy and that is play value.
The kids really liked playing with and collecting Thomas.
So he didn't want much of Thomas outside the specialty
store market. He knew in the small stores or specialty
stores they would treat Thomas as something special and
wouldn't stack it out in bulk. They wouldn't just run it on
an ad and trash the price just to give it away. They would
romance it and keep it special. As a result he didn't want to
really market it with any of the so-called discount stores or
Toys "R" Us. Because he knew we were now competing
hands on with the discounters, he thought we would do the
same thing that they would do. So I went to see Kenn. It
was actually my first time I met Kenn. And we talked about
things and I reminded him that Bob Weinberg, who'd been
with Toys "R" Us for many years and whom Kenn respected, was still a very important part of Toys "R" Us. I gave
him my assurance that we would treat Thomas in a way
that would not only make Toys "R" Us proud but in a way
that he would be proud of. If we didn't, then we would
understand that we didn't deserve to carry the goods. We
talked about how we would do that, that we would give it
dedicated space in the stores, that we wouldn't bulk it out
and try to use it as giveaways. If we advertised it we'd
advertise it based on its being a quality product not that
buy one get one free or anything like that. We would treat
it with a real respect for the brand and try to keep Thomas
as an evergreen product, which it is still today. We would
not promote it like a commodity item or a giveaway item.
We'd promote it and price it based on its value as a toy, as
something the kids played with. So it'd be a reasonable
price, but we wouldn't use price as a way to drive the*

customer in to buy Thomas. We would drive the customer to Thomas based on its play value, its collectability, and we would showcase it in that regard.

We talked for some time then and we shook hands and he said, "All right if you will do that, I'll open the distribution channel to include TRU and only time will tell." We received the goods. We showcased Thomas in our stores and handled it very nicely. We advertised it in accordance with the way we said we would. And it was a wonderful partnership. Anytime Kenn or anyone had any problem with what we did, we looked at it to make sure. A lot of times with all 500 stores, a particular store may not be interpreting our directions properly. We got it corrected and we had a terrific business relationship and a mutual respect. Part of it is when a manufacturer or inventor or licensing agent comes up with a property, it's important to listen to how they want to merchandise and market this property. You can't say OK and then market it or merchandise it in another way because you lose your credibility. I found this to be very important all the time. Your integrity, your credibility is very important. And what is great about working with Kenn is that his word is sacred. If Kenn told you something, it would happen. And he would never go back on his word. You could really trust him. His integrity is outstanding. I think he liked working with me because he felt the same way. And it's not saying that from time to time there would not be a disagreement but it always was resolved in a very professional way and it was never based on anything...it was always a handshake. It's worked out great and from Thomas it also led to some very early exclusive arrangements on Teletubbies.

Most of the things with Thomas, though, were in many ways exclusive because it would be available in the specialty stores, the small stores, and Toys "R" Us. We'd pretty much be the only large store with it. That to me was just as good. Our real competition is Wal-Mart, Target, and Kmart and other stores like them, so if we're the only ones with it, even if several thousand small stores have it, I still consider that a semiexclusive. Which is great. There were Thomas goods that were available to everyone but the broad line on Thomas only Toys "R" Us had, of all the large stores. We also did some special handouts in our stores celebrating that we had Thomas. Things like that to create further interest on the part of our customers.

Customers knew they could now find Thomas in our stores. Now today, it would be different. Today, we would probably put it on our website, and do something special so that way we'd communicate more effectively. Today with E-mails and all kinds of things you can do to communicate one-on-one to customers there's more that we can do.

Because Kenn was very clear in what was important to him, I started to understand how important it was to a license holder or to the inventor and others. It's not only their property it's their baby so to speak. It's something they really believe in and they're counting on you as a retailer to respect the way they want it handled. I learned a lot from that and it's assisted me in dealings with other suppliers or other licensing agents and I think it's helped me understand the business better.

I guess a good example of a licensed property that happened at a similar time that was not handled well was

Barney. What happened with Barney is that there was so much hoopla about Barney, and then the products were not given out to everybody. They were kept very restricted. I think J. C. Penney was the one that had a lot of the Barney clothing and some of the plush and other stores weren't even getting anything. There was a tremendous scarcity and lots of people were upset. Then Lyric Studios [who own Barney] went from that limited distribution to mass production of the product with huge licensing. In other words, you name it, Barney was on it. What they did is overlicense it and made a big mistake. They made a fortune on the way up but then it went down real fast. To their credit the people at Lyric learned from their mistake. They relaunched Barney a few years ago and keep it so that they don't overproduce it. They don't overlicense it and they're keeping Barney alive and well and it's a decent selling item year in year out. If they had handled it differently they probably wouldn't have gotten as big a spike as they did when they got it but I think they could've had a stronger year after year on Barney if they would've used a little more tender loving care of the license. When you give the master toy license to one of the very large toy manufacturer—in the case of Barney it went to Hasbro and in the case of Teletubbies to Hasbro—they want to create volume, and they also want to sell it to all of their major accounts. They want to sell it to everyone but particularly their major accounts. So when Kenn on Thomas the Tank Engine said, wait a minute I don't want it in those discount stores, they're gonna take away from the allure of the product, and kept it where he thought it would be shown *properly. It was bought by the customer not based on price, it was bought based on I want it because it's a terrific toy, my children love playing with it, it's collectible, it's something special, as opposed to Wow! $9.99, I can get it.*

The key to any relationship is communication, right? Well that only gets amplified when you are a small company or a company with limited resources to launch a new product. You need to really listen to your potential partners to understand their needs. From that point you can find a way to make yourself, your company, and/or your product invaluable to them. On the one hand it is true that YOU NEED THEM to launch your product, the most successful way to stay in business with them for the long run is to find a way for THEM TO NEED YOU.

From my conversations with Mike and others at TRU, I learned a great deal about large retailers and the troubles that plagued them. Having a unique product mix from their competitors is a key to their success. It was when we started to talk about exclusive items that I realized how to make our partnership more effective. I realized then that even though we were a small company we could have a big influence in business with this (and any other) huge retailer. Through our dialoguing we learned about each other's needs and concerns and how we could to help one another.

We strive to make sure our communications are one-on-one; however, sometimes we do not have that luxury. When I want to talk to retailers or manufacturers, often I place ads in a variety of trade publications. Creatively the ads are nothing more than a letter to my peers and potential partners from me on my company letterhead. The content however is straight from the heart. Sometimes our ad is a simple thank you, other times we are celebrating a new division, or a new property. And I find it extraordinary how many people send us notes or stop me at a trade show or event to say hey I read your letter it was _____.

The ad layout that we use to sell the properties we market is very straightforward as well. I want the properties to sell themselves. I do not want to be a salesman, anybody can do that. I believe that these properties are truly special and can do a better job selling themselves than anyone else.

Know Your Subject Matter

When communicating about your product, utilize what is going on in the "real" universe and how it effects your audience.

When we started the company, teenage suicides, drug use, dropout rates, and teen violence was on the rise. In fact virtually every negative statistic involving children was on the incline. The government and Hollywood are just coming to the same realization that I made almost 5 years ago: If children are getting most of their messages from the media, isn't it the media's responsibility to provide them with positive messages? It's bad enough that one of the programs with the highest rating of young children is Jerry Springer. (Isn't that awful?) But if the shows that are actually created for young children also promote violent behavior and guns, what does that say about us as a society? And how does it comfort the parents of children who are needless victims of violence? Clearly parents are looking for wholesome alternatives and yet Hollywood keeps churning out megaviolent action films that it promotes to kids. And please don't get me started on Disney's animated film division that markets itself as a children's entertainment group. Their PG-rated movies have more violence and sexual innuendo then many R-rated films. Just because they are animated doesn't mean that their subject matter is appropriate for children.

From listening to our audience, we have established safe*haven* entertainment™. I've always believed that you can provide a program for children that would be fun, funny, and free of gratuitous sexual innuendo and violence, while being enjoyable for them and their caregivers. And every project that we take on must be able to fulfill this very simple requirement. I truly believe that one of the reasons we were able to acquire Eloise (when every major studio in

Hollywood was vying for her) is because we care. Every employee in my company believes that movies/television series for young family audiences do not have to be violent to be entertaining. You will never see us promoting a show, book, movie, or any form of entertainment that allows aggressive behavior. Children (and adults) can get enough of that every day by watching the evening news.

Because it is clear to me that Hollywood has lost its direction with regard to creating strong prosocial theatricals, The itsy bitsy Entertainment Company opened our Los Angeles office on January 1, 1999. The office is headed up by Don Gold, president of Onscreen Entertainment—Theatricals, and is assisted by Robert Kanner, director of acquisitions. Within hours of Robert's first day of working with the company, he mentioned that the rights to Eloise were going to become available. However, I didn't pursue Eloise at that time, because like any reasonable intelligent person, I thought she was going to go to one of the big studios.

And then one day in February, we got a call in our New York office from Simon & Schuster (S&S), who asked if we were interested in representing the licensing rights to the Eloise book series. S&S's subsidiary rights person called, and told us that they were inviting a select number of companies to come up and give them a presentation. Of course, to my surprise, we were invited.

I never use a standardized representation presentation to win a company's confidence that we can do justice to their property. I always encourage my staff to think nontraditionally and usually mention something about the "dynasty philosophy" to them prior to committing to a strategy. I have a lot of questions that they need to answer. Most important, what are their goals? Do they have a vision for their property? Have they started anything that was greeted with some snippet of success? Did they want to do a long-term project with growth over the years or were they more narrowly focused? So I offered to go meet with Simon & Schuster, but not to give them a formal proposal.

During this first meeting, it was clear to me that some of the ideas that they were contemplating were not going to work. The most disconcerting was that Simon & Schuster thought they might parcel off the rights to Eloise. They were thinking of possibly awarding the movie rights to one studio and the merchandising rights to yet another outlet. I knew that this brand was going to need to be managed by one entity if it was to maintain its integrity. I might have mentioned to them at that meeting that the major reason that the Flintstones' movie merchandise was such a disaster was because it was not being handled by one creative center—and of course poor management. The rumor in the licensing industry is that they hired 47 different T-shirt licensees to make product for this one brand, but that is another story (and possibly another book.)

I explained to Simon & Schuster that if they really wanted to keep the brand intact and classic, they had to look at what was best for it long term. It wasn't really about the money they could make initially, but rather the impact they could make long term. Even if it meant that we were not going to represent Eloise, I told them it would be flat out wrong for them to break up the licensing elements and that the brand needed one director regardless if it was book based or theatrically based. I also told them that we could look at Eloise as a whole. It was an interesting meeting, lasting 3 hours, much longer than the original hour they had allotted us.

The negotiation for the rights fell into Don's lap (with me coaching from the sidelines—not that he needed any coaching—Donny went after this project like a coyote that had seen food after not having eaten in several weeks). It was an extraordinary experience to be in negotiations for the rights to Eloise along with the biggest entertainment studios in the world and other well-known and powerful entertainment companies. Let's face it, we had never even made a movie before. Donny had some theatrical experience at Trimark before joining the company, yet The itsy bitsy Entertainment Company was unproven in this arena. We knew that we had to team up with some other entity in order to help our chances of acquiring these rights. Our initial thought was to hook up with a studio. We would acquire the rights and then develop the films with them. We met with a

powerhouse team at one of the studios and worked out the makings
of a deal. At the eleventh hour, the deal they wanted to make with the
property owners and us was so different from what we expected that
we were forced to walk away. At that point, I was pretty sure that we
were out of the bidding. Don called me later that day to tell me that
he had received a call from the William Morris agency.

Apparently Denise Di Novi (the producer of *Edward
Scissorhands, Little Women, Practical Magic, Batman Returns,
Nightmare before Christmas, James and the Giant Peach*, and a
ton more) wanted to meet with us and see if there was something
we could do together on Eloise. She is probably the most creative
and powerful woman producer in Hollywood (and I have since
come to adore her personally as well). After a couple of meetings, it
was abundantly clear that she shared our vision for the movies and
wanted to partner with us. We were back in the race, stronger
and more determined than ever.

The negotiations for Eloise started in February and went on like
a roller-coaster ride until early June. In fact June 8, the night of the
1999 Licensing Awards Gala, as I was on the stage thanking our
industry for the licensing agency of the year award, poor Donny (all
dressed up in a tuxedo) was talking on his cell phone to the attorneys desperately trying to close the deal, while standing in the
kitchen—next to the dishwashers and catering crew. As I was saying thank you so was Donny. This little company that had come
from nowhere had swept the LIMA Awards (the licensing industry's
version of the Oscars) and had won the rights to Eloise basically at
the exact same moment. That was my first time tasting global domination, and from then on there was no turning back.

As soon as it was announced in the papers that Eloise was
ours, Hollywood started calling. The phones have been constantly
ringing and other offers have started to pour in for other projects.
Needless to say, since we acquired those rights, we have experienced
some growing pains. As a result, we have added additional support
staff and are learning how this segment of the industry works. Many
questions have arisen between our new partners and us. All of

which have been cleared up through positive communications and effective expectation management.

Many entertainment companies have told S&S that they were crazy to have chosen my company, and frankly many members of TibECo were hurt by some of the comments. However, on October 12, 1999, it was clear that the Thompson Estate (holders of the rights to Eloise) had chosen the right party to represent their brand.

Simon & Schuster and The itsy bitsy Entertainment Company threw Eloise's Pink & Black Debutante Ball at The Plaza Hotel in New York City. It was vindicating for me to hear Rick Richter, president of Simon & Schuster's Children's Publishing declare "If anyone of you were skeptics just look around the room, you will understand why we chose The itsy bitsy Entertainment Company to entrust with Eloise," in front of our 1500 guests. It confirmed to me that we not only understood their universe, but they had come to an understanding about ours.

Establish Bridges to Your Audience

The marketing portion of the entertainment industry is quite specialized and different from the rest of the industry. As a result, it is always very relieving to hear a partner support our efforts. It is hard for people to grasp that we have so many different entities with which to interact: the property owner, the manufacturer, the media, the creatives, and the retailer. We recognize that the retailer could be either a wall or a doorway, with regards to reaching our audience, so we set out to make friends very early on.

I'm sure you've heard the statement that any company in the business of selling products must understand the retail community they sell to. The fact that every aspect of retailing is always changing—the focus, expectations, promotions, possibilities, and competition—makes it especially challenging for an "outsider" to identify their needs. You need to have your finger on the pulse of it...as much as you can at any given time. During the winter of 1997 we decided that we needed to build relationships with the specialty retailers in order to have a better understanding of their needs. We decided to develop our own brand of toy products exclusively for the specialty stores in order to strengthen our ties with them. We looked as this new challenge as our peace pipe, our offering to sit down and develop relationships with them. This became an extension of our philosophy to make ourselves invaluable to an invaluable part of our business. We wanted to create an environment where the specialty retailer needed us as much as we needed them.

Using our expertise in the preschool toy market, we knew that we could make a toy for the specialty retailer that would be simple and fun, and which would give the retailer solid margins. Headed by Alise Robinson, director of brand development, we established a new division, Hooray! (consumer products). We focused our energies on creating a toy that met all of our requirements. And one day while traveling to a trade show overseas, we found our concept.

We found a product that was made of foam rubber (a derivative of rubber trees—not a synthetic plastic). Alise and I looked at each other and knew that we could take this toy and make the necessary changes to make it work for our needs. And as simple as that, the Huggy Buggy was born (a simple car with a classic engaging shape and a special grip for little hands). Choosing bold primary colors (the colors of the rainbow) would ensure visual stimulation; integrating a special texture would aid sensory development; providing a sturdy shape and wheels would nurture fine and growth motor skill development. And because of its simplicity and fabrication, this toy would be appropriate for children of all ages. We had our product, now we needed to make sure it was what the retailers wanted.

In August 1997 we debuted the Huggy Buggys at the Museum of Modern Art 's store in New York, and then began a slow roll out to reach an initial 30 retailers. This initial exposure enabled us to get a quick reaction and tailor changes before our formal launch at the Toy Fair the following February. Over the past 2 years, the company staffed up with the ever-essential sales, marketing and financial arms. Hooray! has developed into a profitable business (they have more than quintupled initial sales since the first year and are now in over one thousand doors) through continually understanding their customers needs and being responsive to them. The Huggy Buggy was originally packaged in a die-cut package that could be "pegged" at retail. (Visual A) The feedback was clear—the packaging was not conducive to a clean retail presentation. The packaging got torn and consumers didn't display just how delicious the cars were. Alise looked at the packaging challenge with a keen eye and saw an opportunity to provide the "presentation" for the retailers. "License plate" hangtags were created for the cars and Lucite dump bins were offered to accounts (Visual B). This worked especially well for the chain specialty accounts, but not for the mom and pop stores, because much of the product was getting dirty. Taking a step back to look at her focus, Alise saw that offering a carrying case that stored the toy (Visual C) would be a solution for retailers and at the same time have added value for children.

How Strong Is Your Foundation?

Because we were so busy creating/marketing great stuff for kids, I didn't notice how my own company was growing in both size and stature. In the spring of 1999 I realized that my little family had grown into a medium-sized corporation. We had offices in five different locations in three countries (and more planned), and although we were extremely efficient, further growth was inevitable. The demands on the company were increasing and yet our corporate structure had not. There were certain things that were not getting done, whereas others were being done by several people at the same time. Some of the employees were taking on too much; others not taking on enough. And I personally was spending too much time on the minutiae. It was time to take a step back and take a critical look at our corporate structure. The thing is that I know we needed more structure and yet I was unable to see how best to make the changes. Sort of like the saying, you can't see the

Visual A

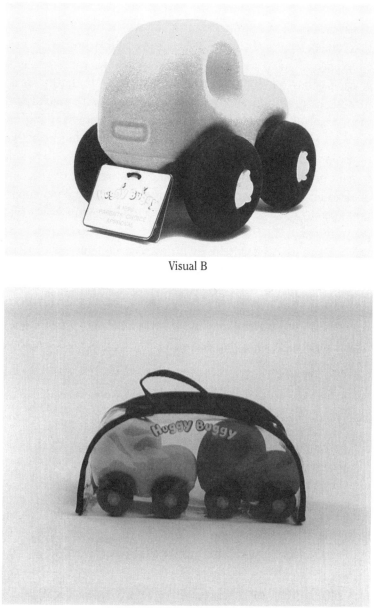

Visual B

Visual C

forest for the trees. We needed a fresh perspective and a fresh eye, so we called in a management consultant whom Dean knew, to talk to us and help initiate change. This was not an easy process. I needed to open up my company to a total stranger and ask him to look at each of my 50 employees and evaluate their strengths, weaknesses, and needs. I needed to have him sit down with each department head and work with them to figure out what was working and not working within their own areas, and with their business relationships inside and outside their specific areas. I needed to be able to shift people's responsibilities without allowing them to become dissatisfied or disillusioned. I knew this was too big and too important a job to allow my ego or Dean's (COO) or Josephine's (CAO) to get in the way. The fact is that we did not have the resources to do this job and we needed help. By hiring a consultant, and working with him, we had an expert who could guide us and put all of our visions into focus. What we were able to accomplish by this 3-month-long exercise was to build a workable business model that would be able to accommodate my company's future growth, without changing the core that sets us apart. We made some specific statements:

Niche doesn't necessarily equal small:
> The itsy bitsy Entertainment Company has a clear focus on the preschool market, but that market takes into account everything and anything that might be done for that age group and the people that care for and love them.

Know when to go for help and who to go to:
> We know that our focus is making really great things for the youngest of children and those who care for them, but sometimes we don't have all the answers. If there is a crisis, we know that there are experts we can count on, and we've identified them so we can get their opinions and advice. Just as you wouldn't go to a general practitioner when you need a specialist, you can't expect to be able to provide all the answers all the time. It's OK to say, I don't know, but I'll find out and get back to you.

Hire the best, at all costs:
> This is simple. Put your efforts into putting together the best staff, the best vendors, the best support you can afford, even at your own personal expense. It will more than pay off in the long run.

Provide more than just customer service:
> Any company can put on a help line, but it's the people you put on those lines and the ownership they take in helping your customers and your clients that counts. You need to give people the tools with which to serve your community.

Look at every situation as a unique opportunity and tailor your strategies to meet and exceed expectations:
> You cannot provide cookie-cutter solutions to every situation and think that it will work to your advantage. The only rule is that there must be an effort made to understand the people or commodity that you work with, what makes it unique and what you can contribute to make it better.

Read everything you can about your business niche, and immerse yourself in it. That means if you are doing great things for children, get to understand them, spend time with them, ask them questions and listen to their answers. Spend the time to get to know your employees and make sure that each of your department heads gets to know each of theirs. It is so very important during a time of large impersonal corporations to make sure that you can make your corporate culture a safe place where people feel comfortable trying new things, while adhering to the systems in place, and taking chances to enable your company to move ahead. That means you as a leader and everyone you entrust as your representative.

Work with your staff, allow them to take on the training necessary to learn more about their job, and do that yourself. Just because you head the area or the company does not mean that you can't learn how to make yourself a better contributor to the whole.

Just saying I do great things for children doesn't mean I understand what those things should be. There is a big difference

between a 2-year-old and a 6-year-old. I need to be able to understand what their social, cognitive, and learning skills are and find a
way to fill these needs. They are my end consumers, and I need to
know what makes them tick, just as you do with your end consumer. Understanding your universe will offer you the door in
which to enter your home....

1. How would you define your business universe?
2. What companies are in this universe?
3. How would you define your end user's universe?
4. What resources (publications, trade shows, seminars) will help
   you keep you up to date with changes in your industry and
   with your end user?

   Your business universe is:_____
   and your end user's universe is: _____

Making Leaders Out of Your Followers

Heroes shape us and role models make us.

I think one of the big mistakes that many people make in business is that they let their egos get in the way. Everyone wants to take credit for everyone else's work and most employees are not included in the overall project, just one aspect of the total picture. It is really important to finds ways to motivate your employees and to take at least some of the responsibility to make them more productive. Fear of losing a job or dangling money in front of an employee is not going to create long-term motivation. Think of this concept as a pyramid—no matter how big your followers are—by definition whoever sits on the top is always going to be bigger. If you want to be bigger, then make your followers big.

Apparently, I have an unorthodox approach to working with my staff. I try to be there for them both on a personal level as well as a professional level and I try to help manage our expectations of each other. I want them to not only own part of their world, but I want them to feel they are part of mine as well. Above all else I try to be both a mentor and a role model for them.

As I mentioned in the prologue, I was influenced from an early age by feature films and television. One of my favorite characters in popular movie culture is *Auntie Mame*. She was an original who had extraordinary compassion. Auntie Mame was a determined woman who was often misunderstood yet nothing stopped her from attaining her goals. Above all else, she was in a constant state of change while never losing her focus. When I was growing up, I must have seen that movie 50 times. As embarrassing as this is to admit, I have often thought of myself as a male version of Auntie Mame (Uncle Kenn). She clearly affected my psyche, because she understood people and their basic needs.

From an early age, there have been many people in my life that have impacted my way of thinking. Other than members of my family like my dad and my Grandpa Moishe, my friend Richie was my first role model.

When I was in the third grade, a new family moved in across the street. They had a son my age, Richie Filler, and for several years (until his family moved away) he was my best friend. It could have been a real drag to have your best friend be the biggest, smartest, funniest and best athlete in the school, and somehow it wasn't. Anything I could do, Richie could do better, but he never made me feel inferior. I realize that this sounds silly, but think about how many kids you know that have that degree of humility. He had a lot of power over the other kids, he was definitely the leader of the pack and yet he was gracious, compassionate, and kind. Richie always tried to teach me what he knew, or show me how to do something (like play basketball better—I was a hopeless case, but he never gave up). He was patient, and I was always learning something from him. And I actually did get better than him at a couple of things (not basketball). Although I haven't spoken to Richie (who is probably "Richard" now) in close to 25 years, I still learn things from those years with him. Just because someone is the leader doesn't make him or her better or more important. Richie taught me that everyone has value and if you believe in others they will believe in you.

Since the third grade, I have met literally hundreds of people and I have tried to learn from them and give to them at the same time. I have learned that everyone you meet has something to share and to teach. Even the worst situations have something to teach.

Several years prior to opening my company, I had a rather unpleasant experience that reinforced for me the importance of caring for others, and how important it is for a "manager" to get "personal' with their "staff."

I went to graduate school to specialize in industrial psychology, a relatively obscure degree almost 20 years ago. Without getting into the how's and why's of it, I can honestly say that it was absolutely the worst time of my life. It was a horrible situation. The irony is that my professors were there to teach us about making companies healthier by working closer with the individual employee, and yet they had no idea how to put these concepts to work in their daily lives.

The concept of industrial psychology is basically dealing with sick businesses instead of sick people. Therefore the concepts often focus around the concepts of employees' motivation and productivity: If you can help an employee to sort out their personal problems you will make them more motivated and ultimately more productive at work.

Unfortunately, the professors at the school I was enrolled in knew the textbook definition of things, but had no idea how to put them into practice and certainly did not make it a part of their everyday life. Of the 15 or so students enrolled in my class only about 5 survived till the end of the first semester. My roommate (a friend from undergrad) was having so much trouble adjusting to the stress and anxiety of the program that he actually suffered some type of nervous breakdown (right in front of my eyes). When I asked the teachers to intervene, they simply looked at me dumbfounded as if to say that they were just teachers and that this was none of their business. As if it were yesterday, I clearly remember my roommate getting in front of the class prepared to do his oral report and then suddenly a couple of men in white coats came to take him away (I don't know if I saw a straightjacket or just imagined one later—it was 20 years ago). No explanation or conversation ensued with the teachers and the students and not one of the professors asked if I was all right after seeing my roommate and dear friend dragged away. In fact we never spoke of it again. When my roommate was escorted out of the room, the only thing the professor said was something to the effect of "(student name) it's your turn to present." A couple of days afterward, the head of the psychology department told me that they had been monitoring my roommate's behavior for several days/weeks (he never asked how I was coping or anything else about me personally for that matter). He further explained that my roommate was being released and that I should not go back to my apartment for a few days. Nor was I to have any communication with him or I would be facing possible removal from the program.

And I (being a good sheep) did what I was told, regardless of how poorly the school managed this situation. It was obviously a very emotional time for me and I was not thinking clearly. To this day, I still feel guilty about how I treated my roommate and wonder if I did the right thing by not being there for him—and if he is OK.

I learned a few things both by what they taught in the classroom and by what they didn't practice out of the classroom. The most interesting of which was that to motivate people and make them more productive, you need to help them deal with what is affecting their emotional state outside the workplace. How unfortunate that the professors didn't understand how to internalize these concepts. I have had an open-door policy for as long as I have been a manager. My staff knows that they can talk to me about anything—and I do mean anything. We have had some real obscure conversations over the past 5 years that have helped my staff regain their focus and their productivity.

Common Goals/Common Enemies

After spending years at getting it wrong, I now realize what most employees want and need out of their working experience. Simply put, all they want is an equal amount of authority to responsibility. They want to be respected and appreciated and they want to be part of a team effort. Most companies, on the other hand, want to wipe out their competition and be the dominant players in their field. These two apparently unrelated issues need to come together in order to establish a long-term successful business.

This is where the concept of common enemy/common goal comes into play. And it is a relevant concept whether a person is trying to pick up someone in a bar, whether it is the government going to war, or whether it is someone trying to launch a new product into the market. With Combat the cockroach killer—obviously the common enemy and the common goal are one in the same—the total elimination of cockroaches. With a new television series like the *Teletubbies* or *It's itsy bitsy Time!* the common goal or common enemy formula is not as easy to recognize (common goal—to create a healthy environment for children on the television screen; common enemy—violence). Both our employees and our audience believe in these values and that is why these programs have become popular.

Many managers don't understand that the "common goal/common enemy principle" is the most effective tool in motivation and productivity. They tend to think that money is the great motivator. However, money only serves as a bandage—a short-term temporary solution. After time (and usually a rather short time), the quick fix of the salary increase or the raise is gone and now the employee is back on the doorstep looking for more money, feeling as though he or she deserves a new salary and looking for more. With the concept of common goals/common enemies the employee tends to be motivated for a much longer period of time.

At TibECo we are constantly redefining our common goals for ourselves, within the company and for our partners. We both have smaller benchmark goals that are along the road to our bigger goal of global domination. In late 1998, we sat down together as a company and discussed a plan to sweep the industry's licensing awards. We looked at all of the possible categories and developed a plan for each individual category.

As far as the "enemy" is concerned, when you're a small company you always have some enemy: creators of unhealthy children's products or big Hollywood studios who don't consider the needs of the caregiver or other producers of entertainment. I think that a little competition is healthy in business and I try to come up with new challenges for the company.

In order for us to succeed, I know that I have to keep us thinking together. Every employee needs to know that he or she has something to add—even if it's not directly a part of the job responsibility. I believe that most people have the potential to be leaders. The question is, Do they believe in themselves? I can usually discover this when we interview them.

During the interview process, one of the questions we ask is, "Besides your specific work experience, what other qualities or skills do you bring to the party?" Now, I realize that this is really a nontraditional approach to interviewing but it works for me. Even though most résumé books tell you not to mention any hobbies, etc., just in case the potential boss has an aversion. For example, in publishing, some bosses would never hire someone who is a poet. It always amazes me what people have to offer, from flower arranging to origami to playing the guitar. One of our staff members is an actor, one worked for an ad firm, and yet another was a preschool teacher. I believe that this approach to interviewing gives an employer an insight into the likes and dislikes of an employee. If you can incorporate some of their interests into their workday then they could be more motivated employees. You would not believe how handy these talents and skills have been to our company. We have written our own songs, created "play days" for retailers, and created our own advertising design and layout. It is really important to find out what people know how to do well and what they like to do (you may find that what they like to do and what they are good at have nothing to do with each other). Sometimes you can give your employees the opportunity to work on things that are not part of their job descriptions for their own personal satisfaction and help round them out more as people.

In the early days of our company, many of the employees in the company wore many hats. In one case, we took on a very ambitious project to manufacture dolls for a property we represented. We had a great deal of experience directing manufacturers; however, we had never made products for ourselves. Two of our employees, Josephine Interrante, now our chief administrative officer, and Dean asked if they could be part of the production team, even though neither of them had ever made a toy product before. Because they both worked in the operations side of the business, I knew that they understood the profit structure module. However the concept of working on the roll out of product, from delivery dates to order quantities, even which product at which time of year, would be a new challenge for them. The idea that they were actually touching product and working on which colors and fabrications, was very rewarding for me and a great learning experience for them. Dean and Josephine garnered an understanding of the product development process and what skills are needed to create great stuff. Since then both Dean and Josephine have used this information through the years. Josephine uses her knowledge in the hiring process, and Dean is better able to do budget projections. This experience was invaluable for the two of them.

Allowing your employees the luxury of having new experiences that provide them with the opportunity to grow not only on a business level—but also on a personal level—will generate a more enthusiastic staff. In the case of my company, it helps raise the level of creative energy around the office. Most business people know on an intellectual level that ideas can come from anywhere within their company; however, few create an environment for that to happen with their lower-level employees. A bolt of inspiration can come to anyone from an art exhibit or a magazine or at the grocery checkout isle. It would be a lost opportunity to not utilize all of the energies that surround your business—and I hate lost opportunities.

Creative Inspiration

The key is to integrate these opportunities into your business. It's amazing how much more employees have to offer when they realize that you want them to have something to offer. Alana Shaw was hired as our company's receptionist a few years ago. One day, we put out an E-mail telling everyone that we were looking for a name for a product that Alise and I were working on. We were all set to call the vehicles the "Bouncy Buggys"; however, neither Alise nor I really liked the name. Suddenly, Alana said why don't you call them the Huggy Buggys instead. Alise and I looked at each other and gave Alana a big hug and went about changing all of the creatives, including the packaging to adopt this new warmer brand name. As a little side note, Alana has been promoted twice now and works within the publishing division of our business—quid pro quo.

It is virtually impossible to come up with a formula to increase productivity in an employee. This is because outside factors interfere with employees' abilities to focus and concentrate on their work. The best way I know to motivate my staff is not to threaten their jobs if they make a mistake; in fact it is just the opposite. I need my staff to know that they are loved and respected and I do not chastise them for getting it wrong. I try to give them an environment where they feel safe to take risks and challenge themselves. If employees are constantly in fear of losing their jobs, they are going to be preoccupied and are not likely to be particularly creative in their thinking—playing it safe never does lead to global domination.

Four Prongs of Leadership

Dean has a *four*-pronged concept of leadership. He says that before a person can become a leader that person must take *ownership* for his/her work as well as be *responsible* for bringing the company closer to its goals. On a regular basis, Dean sits down with employees and asks them about their current projects. He wants an update and wants to know what proactive steps that employee is taking to achieve our goals. We do not allow others to pass the buck at our company. If something goes wrong it is everyone's fault not one individual's. Many companies take only one or the other of these into account, when reviewing an employee's performance. In addition to accountability and responsibility, Dean's other two prongs are *accountability* and *empowerment*. Just like with a diamond ring, you need all four prongs in place to hold the stone securely.

Ownership is defined in the dictionary as "a person who owns something as his property" and empowerment is "to give power or authority to." These definitions are not descriptive enough for me in a business environment. What is missing for me is, How did the person obtain what he or she owns? What do they envision it to be? Do they want it to grow because they are given the responsibility for nurturing it? It is important for the manager of a business to empower his/her employees to make decisions and to give them a piece of the business or product to manage. The fear is that the employee will get too big for their britches and will create more harm than good. My experience is that employees only want to be appreciated. They are not likely to deliberately step over the line—and will come to their boss if they think the decision they need to make is too big for them alone.

Once employees have been given both the ownership and responsibility of clear assignments, they need to be empowered by being given all of the tools they need to succeed, and then they need to be held accountable for their success. We tend, as managers, not to give our employees all of the information they need to succeed on their own. Sometimes it is out of insecurity and other times it is because we are too busy to spend the time. If we don't spend the time up front, we are going to spend twice as much time correcting the situation later. As for the insecurities, we have to remember that no matter how big your "junior" gets, you are always by definition bigger. I use my best efforts to make sure that my employees are as well rounded and as "big"as possible.

In most companies, after the licensing people make the deal, the creative department takes over on the product development and the launch of the products at retail. In our company, however, the licensing people not only negotiate the deal, they are also actively involved in every aspect of the product development, from the initial product concepts, to product approval, through to production, packaging and advertising, and promotion at retail. I do not allow them to be assembly-line workers (not that there is anything wrong with assembly-line workers).

Laura Spector, our Hasbro liaison, not only makes the deal with the manufacturer, but works with them and the creators in developing each item in the line, the catalogs, the sell sheets, the print and on-air advertising, the packaging, and introducing the product to the marketplace. Everything from concept through to implementation. I ask her to participate in each step of the process, because I want her to be empowered, responsible, accountable, and have some ownership in the product's success at retail. As a result of this process, I believe that our toy products come out better (more consistent) and our staff takes greater pride in their personal accomplishments. Of course, there are guidelines. Prior to developing products, I sit down with the category manager and ask them the following questions:

> *Does this work for the end user?*
> *Will it make a child smile?*
> *Is it right for the property?*
> *Is it an extension of the creator's original intenet?*
> *Is it something new and creative?*

My experience suggests that the single most effective way to make employees productive is to share your commitment with them and to make them part of that vision. This sharing process gets harder and harder as we add on more employees. In the early days, there were so few of us that we had lunch together everyday. That was our "meeting" time. We bought packaged pasta down the street for two dollars and made lunch for the staff. We developed a family atmosphere that allowed us to talk openly with one another about anything from our work lives or our personal lives. This openness helped create an environment where everyone had something invested in everyone else. An extra special teamwork developed which has become a cornerstone to our success. As we grew, the challenge was how to keep that close-knit feeling.

Initially, we made the whole company a part of the hiring process. With so few people in the company this was pretty easy. Josephine, Dean, and I would put faces to the résumés. When we were serious about making a candidate an offer, we'd ask him or her to our office for lunch. At these lunches, I would ask the entire company to talk about when they started and what they liked best and least about working for The itsy bitsy Entertainment Company. I did this for two reasons. First, I wanted the potential employee to know what they were getting into, both the good and the bad, because I had goals and I needed the people we hired to be committed to achieving them. The second reason was to give me insight into what was working at the company—what was motivating people. After the "contestant" left the office we would take a vote. Everyone, and I mean *everyone,* had to unanimously agree to take responsibility for this person or we would not hire him or her. Believe it or not people have failed lunch. The last lunch was with the twenty-third person hired. We just got too big and too busy. We have started the process again, now the individual departments meet the prospective employee and then they vote.

Because of our staff size, the expense, and the scheduling, it became extremely difficult to continue our companywide staff

lunches. Now we have replaced the lunches with my famous 9:00
A.M. meetings. As appropriate, the entire company will get in one of
the conference rooms or on conference calls and we'll talk about a
variety of things ranging from a new success to general concerns or
just to meet the newest members of the company.

With almost 60 employees, we now go to much greater (and
costlier) lengths to keep the family spirit alive. On a quarterly basis
the entire company from all of our offices (New York, Los Angeles,
Toronto, Washington, DC, São Paolo, and soon Munich) meet for
some type of social function. These events are exclusive to employees with the only exception being at our winter party where all the
employees are actually encouraged to bring someone from their
personal lives with them.

To celebrate our anniversary each year (the ides of March),
we've held a special "itsy bitsy black tie event with a twist." The
events have ranged from black tie bowling to flying everyone to
Los Angeles for our office opening. Everyone thinks I'm crazy, and
yet I know that they look forward to seeing what we are going to
do next year. We work as a team and we play as a team. We all recognize how important it is to have everyone personally buy into
the dream, so it is important for everyone to get to know each
other out of the office environment. Senior staff and junior staff,
the art department, and the accounting department, those who
had been at the company the longest with those who had just
started all engaged in some fun nonwork-related activity. It gives
them an opportunity to ask questions, get to know each other and
just get a different perspective of their personal contribution to
TibECo. It also provides extraordinary teambuilding exercises for
the entire company.

In the summer, we always schedule a summer play day—"The
itsy bitsy mystery adventure." The first time we did this was in
1998, everyone came into New York and we rented a bus and went
to my house in the country. This year the entire company went on
a mystery trip to Teletubbyland. Next year we will go somewhere
else that requires a passport.

We have an annual holiday party, where each staff member is asked to bring someone—a husband, wife, boyfriend, girlfriend, their elementary school teacher, or other acquaintance. During one holiday event, we asked everyone to share one thing they had never told anyone. Several people told us about strange jobs or other silly things from their childhood. Some of the declarations were truly funny and others were more serious. One spouse had a secret that she was keeping from her husband. It surprised everyone, especially the person's spouse, when she confessed that she had lied about her College Board scores in order to get a job. I've learned a great deal about our own employees from the things that their friends shared—in fact we all have.

We had so much fun playing the "tell me something I don't know about you game," at our winter party that we played it at a first introductory meeting with one of our new clients. A very straight-laced senior executive working for my partner confessed that prior to her joining her company, she had spent a few months on stage as a magician's assistant. When she told us, we all starting laughing—it certainly was an icebreaker. I have never been able to look at her exactly the same way since. Somehow whenever you open up and share a bit about yourself or your dreams with your coworkers, and ask them to do the same, it breaks down certain barriers. Not to mention, how to blackmail them in the future (only kidding).

Part of making leaders out of your followers is giving them the opportunity to manage your expectations. Every employee who has joined The itsy bitsy Entertainment Company has been given a copy of "the TibECo bible" that not only explains our benefits, holidays and vacation policies, but also provides them with an insight about our focus. Each new employee must understand that they are about to embark on an exciting journey into the minds of the youngest of children. Their new job will be to make the world a happier place for itsy-bitsys everywhere. They will need to follow up every caregiver's inquiry within 24 hours. We must put our clients, customers, and the general public first and never lose sight of our audience. Those are the same standards that have remained since the day TibECo hired its first employee. I know it sounds a little spooky to talk so fanatically, and yet I must get people who share the same mission.

WWKD

I was fortunate to have been able to bring my key management team up by working closely with them on a day-to-day basis. We were able to immerse ourselves in our projects and made choices that may not have been the most popular ones, but that stayed true to our mission. After several years, my core group of key managers have been able to share my vision with their staffs. As a joke they started to ask themselves "WWKD" when faced with a tough decision. The WWKD stood for "What would Kenn do?" (how embarrassing to put that in writing). Their ability to predict my thoughts and actions has allowed me to continue to expand the company with the faith that my senior management team would keep things on track. Of course I am still very actively involved and available. From time to time, I have to remind myself that developing key leaders means entrusting them with your vision, once you have provided them with all the tools. It is the only way the company will continue to grow, and it also allows others to take a special pride in their accomplishments.

TRUST

By having people go through this process, we give them ownership in every aspect of their work and the reward of seeing their own dream become a reality. It is vital to make sure that your employees have an equal amount of responsibility and authority. Often we give employees the responsibility to get something done, but we do not give them the authority to make the necessary decisions/choices to get the job done. If employees have to come in and get approved to do each step of the process then they are likely to not make any proactive choices and just wait for you to give them their next set of instructions. This is certainly not going to make a leader out of anyone. In fact it is more likely to create the exact opposite effect. People need to know that they are trusted to make the right call. It is important that the manager gives their employees a project that they can master and is there to give guidance, when requested, but is not there to smother and dominate.

I began the book with a chapter on focus and it is only fitting that I bring it full circle in this last chapter. Focus gives you the opportunity to stay on course even when you are being pulled in a million different directions. It allows your employees and partners to understand where you are coming from and learn how to work with you. It is the foundation with which you build your house. Giving ownership to your followers is the door which allows them the freedom explore the world around them while having the safety of coming back to your home.

This last workshop will allow you to complete the building of your own house, provide you with a back door for another way to enter and explore your world, and let your goals become a reality.

1. What do you need to be doing to move your business forward?
   _____

2. What projects are prohibiting you from doing what you need to do to move your business forward? _____

3. What are the five elements most important to you in order to accomplish the projects the way you would do them? _____
   _____
   _____
   _____
   _____
   _____

The people you delegate to need to understand these elements most important to you, as the list defines.

Epilogue

I have always believed that everyone has a book and a song within him or her. I just had no idea that my book was about business (at least I hope my song is about love—can you imagine a club mix to "global domination"?). My life has been blessed with great opportunities that I have been ready to exploit at the right time. All I needed was a strong belief and a commitment to see it through. I am excited about the future and possibilities it brings with it. My personal motto is "Be ready to pounce."

Now that you've gone through the stages of building a virtual business with me, I hope that you will view things a bit differently. Keep in mind that you need to build a strong foundation through your focus. Your walls need to support the managing of expectations of others; separating believers from nonbelievers; thinking out of the box and knowing who your end user is. Your roof of promotion protects your house, and you have a way in and out by understanding you universe and by making leaders out of your followers.

Use the outcome of your exercises to create your own home. Fill in the bricks with what is unique about your own business or ideas and then put them to work. Remember if you cannot take on the globe as it is then make a smaller one and dominate it instead.

About the Author

Kenn Viselman is founder and Chairman of The itsy bitsy Entertainment Company. A maverick in the world of children's entertainment, he has made his mark working on some of the most successful children's brands in history. Viselman divides his time between his homes in New York and LA with his dog, Baldwin.